9/10 LHC

Grammar Wise 1

Kevin Anthony Keating
University of Arizona, Tucson

New Readers Press

Grammar Wise 1
ISBN 978-1-56420-430-1

Copyright © 2004 New Readers Press
New Readers Press
A Publishing Division of ProLiteracy
1320 Jamesville Avenue, Syracuse, New York 13210
www.newreaderspress.com

Printed in the United States of America
9   8   7   6   5   4   3   2

All proceeds from the sale of New Readers Press materials
support literacy programs in the United States and worldwide.

Acquisitions Editor: Paula L. Schlusberg
Content Editor: Judi Lauber
Production Manager: Andrea Woodbury
Designer: Andrea Woodbury
Illustrations: Kirsten Lindquist
Production Specialist: Jeffrey R. Smith
Cover Design: Andrea Woodbury

Contents

About This Book

Grammar Wise 1 is designed to teach basic grammar to beginning-level ESL students. The text is appropriate for class use, homework, and independent study. The grammatical structures build progressively throughout the book, yet units are independent. Teachers can begin at any point, use the units in any order, and recycle topics or activities that students still need to master.

After introducing basic use of nouns, adjectives, prepositions, and the verb *be, Grammar Wise 1* moves on to count and noncount nouns; indefinite articles; present, past, and present progressive tenses; and the modals *can* and *will.* Many exercises include questions and answers so that students can practice conversation and question formation.

Each unit of *Grammar Wise 1* focuses on a particular grammatical structure, but also recycles structures and vocabulary from earlier units. Each unit uses models, rather than formal rules, to introduce the target structure. At this level, it is not necessary to explicitly teach rules for a structure. Instead, use the model sentences to draw attention to key features. Students can read and repeat the models and suggest other sentences that use the structure before moving on to the exercises.

The Grammar Handbook in Appendix 2 (pages 177–204) supplements these brief introductions for students who can use more detailed explanations. The Handbook provides rules for each structure, including additional details of usage, common errors, and exceptions.

The exercises allow students to internalize new structures and contrast them with structures learned earlier. In each unit, exercises advance from recognition to production and from controlled answers to free expression. This progression helps students assimilate new material and move toward mastery.

Similar kinds of exercises are repeated throughout the text. This repetition allows students to become familiar with what an exercise requires so that they can focus on the grammatical structure and can function more independently in class. Suggestions for conducting the activities, as well as specific suggestions for each unit, are presented in the *Grammar Wise Teacher's Guide.*

Dictation exercises, included in all units except Introductory Unit A, provide a controlled aural introduction to the target structure. The sentences for dictation are provided in Appendix 1 (pages 171–176). Most units also include an error-correction exercise, which helps students develop editing skills.

Many exercises are followed by discussion questions related to topics or information from the exercise. These discussions can be whole-class activities, but they also provide excellent opportunities for students to practice natural conversation in pairs or small groups. The questions are designed to elicit structures and vocabulary from the exercise, personalizing use of the structures by asking students about their own experience. At this level, short answers are appropriate. A single word or a simple "yes" or "no" may be all that some students can produce, especially in early units. Other students will respond more elaborately. When possible, encourage students to expand their answers and, when they talk with a partner, to ask for more details. Model and teach suitable follow-up questions.

Exercise items draw on topics relevant to students' lives and interests. Many relate to geography, nature, weather, history, and human behavior. Other items draw on students' experiences, for example, with food, sports, entertainment, work, and education. Some items ask about people in students' lives, such as their classmates, neighbors and friends, co-workers, and family members. If a student does not have the relative or person referred to, replace the term, or guide the student in adapting the response. For example, a student could say, "I don't have a brother," or tell about a different person: "I don't have a brother, but my sister has black hair."

Grammar Wise 1 is designed to take students beyond the mechanical study of grammar. It personalizes practice and helps students relate the material to their language needs outside class. The activities provide many opportunities to share personal information, encouraging meaningful interactions that promote both learning and natural language use.

Review of Alphabet and Spelling

Room 209
Ms. Susan McFarland

How do you spell your name?

Capital Letters

A	B	C	D	E	F	G	H	I	J	K	L	M
N	O	P	Q	R	S	T	U	V	W	X	Y	Z

Small Letters

a	b	c	d	e	f	g	h	i	j	k	l	m
n	o	p	q	r	s	t	u	v	w	x	y	z

An Important Question

How do you spell _____?
Example: How do you spell your name?

Exercise 1

Ask your teacher, "How do you spell your name?" Write the name.

My teacher's name: _____

Exercise 2

Ask your partner, "How do you spell your name?" Write the name.

My partner's name: _____

Exercise 3

Some students will spell their names. Write their names.

1. _____
2. _____
3. _____
4. _____

Exercise 4

Your teacher will name things in the room. Ask, "How do you
spell _____?" Write the words.

1. _____
2. _____
3. _____
4. _____

Exercise 5

Ask your partner, "How do you spell your home city or country?"
Write the name.

My partner's home city or country: _____

Exercise 6

Some students will spell their home city or country. Write the names.

1. _____

2. _____

3. _____

4. _____

Exercise 7

Your teacher will give you a word. Spell the word for your partner.
Your partner will write the word. Your partner will spell a word.
Write the word.

My partner's word: _____

Exercise 8

Some students will spell their words. Write the words.

1. _____

2. _____

3. _____

4. _____

Exercise 9

Write a word on each line. Your teacher will check your spelling.
Discuss as a class.

1. a food: _____

2. a car: _____

3. a country: _____

4. an animal: _____

5. a sport: _____

B Four Important Questions

How do you pronounce this word?

Meaning

What does _____ mean?

Spelling

How do you spell _____?

Pronunciation

How do you pronounce _____?

Translation

How do you say _____ in (language)?

Exercise 1: Meaning

Look at each picture. Write a question about the meaning of the word.

1. button: _What does "button" mean?_

2. toe: _____

3. wink: _____

4. broom: _____

Exercise 2: Spelling

Your teacher will read a word. Ask, "How do you spell _____?" Write the word. Then write your question about the spelling of the word.

1. _____right_____   _How do you spell "right"?_
2. _____   _____
3. _____   _____
4. _____   _____
5. _____   _____

Exercise 3: Pronunciation

Write a question about the pronunciation of each word.

1. cough: _How do you pronounce "cough"?_
2. building: _____
3. sword: _____
4. clouds: _____
5. laugh: _____

Exercise 4: Translation

Write a question about the translation of each word. Then ask a classmate.

1. goodbye: _How do you say "goodbye" in Spanish?_
2. hello: _____
3. friend: _____
4. yes: _____
5. teacher: _____

Exercise 5

Choose your own words. Write questions. Then ask your classmates.

1. meaning: _____
2. spelling: _____
3. pronunciation: _____
4. translation: _____

Basic Punctuation

C

Is Ms. Delgado a student, or does she have a job?

Capital Letters

A B C D E F G H I J K L M N O P Q R S T U V W X Y Z

Examples: My name is Sanda.
The capital of Korea is Seoul.
Mr. Popp speaks English and French.
May I help you?
We have class Monday through Friday.
Titanic is a long movie.

Period .

Examples: Dr. Lee
the U.S.
That is a good book.
$10.50
a.m./p.m.

Comma ,

Examples: March 15, 1978
275,000,000
Austin, Texas
Bangkok, Thailand

Question Mark ?

Examples: How are you?
What time is it?

Dollar Sign $

Examples: $25
$42.50

Colon :

Examples: 8:30
1:20 a.m.

Exercise 1: Dictation

Listen to your teacher. Write the sentences. Check your capital letters and punctuation.

1. _____ is _____

2. _____ is _____ today

3. _____ time _____

4. It's _____

5. _____ teacher's name is _____

6. _____ first language is _____

7. _____ gallon of gasoline is _____

Exercise 2

Circle the correct words. Check for capital letters and punctuation.

1. ((Venezuela) venezuela) is in (South America (South America.))

2. (the   The) door is not (open   Open   open.   Open.)

3. (Are   Are?   are   are?) you (american?   American   American?)

4. (Albert   albert) is from (germany   germany.   Germany.)

5. (today   Today) is not (December, 25, 2002.   December 25, 2002.)

6. (Mrs.   Mrs   mrs.) Wong is not a (teacher.   teacher   Teacher.)

Discuss

a. What is another country in South America?
b. What is the date today?
c. Is anyone in your family a teacher?

Exercise 3

Fix any mistakes.

1. Our teacher is from ᴀustralia.

2. spanish is the language of mexico

3. How are you

4. He is 52 years old.

5. anya went to Paris France

6. Is it a good Movie

7. Mr. thompsen died on april 3 1997.

8. that computer costs 1000$.

9. This is a japanese car

10. Our textbook is *grammar wise 1.*

Exercise 4

Write the answers. Check for capital letters and punctuation. Discuss the answers with a partner.

1. today's date: _____

2. the time now: _____

3. your complete name: _____

4. your father's and mother's first names: _____

5. your birthday: _____

6. your home city and country: _____

7. the capital of your home country: _____

8. your nationality: _____

9. the leader of your home country: _____

10. your first language: _____

11. the cost of your book: _____

12. a famous book or movie: _____

13. a big company: _____

14. a question for your classmate: _____

15. a question for your teacher: _____

Questions and Question Words

Who? What? Where? When? Why? How?

Question Words

who
what
where
when
why
how
which
what time
what color
how old
how much
how many

Questions and Answers

Examples: Are you a student? Yes.
Is Panama a very big country? No.
Are you from Korea or from Japan? Japan.
Is Egypt in Africa or Asia? It is in Africa.
Who is your teacher? Our teacher is Mr. Hoffman.
What is your name? My name is Alicia.
When is your birthday? October 15.
Where do you live? I live on Mountain Drive.
Why are you so happy? Because the weather is beautiful.
Which sport do you like best? I like basketball.
Do you like jazz? Yes. (or) No.

Exercise 1

Read each question. Circle the answer.

1. Who is he? (It is my car. He is Mr. Enciso. He is fine.)

2. What is your favorite food?
   (It is at 7:00 p.m.   He is my father.   It is chicken and rice.)

3. Where is the bank? (It is on Main Street.   It is tomorrow.   It is OK.)

4. When is the class? (Yes, it is.   It is in Room 205.   It is on Friday.)

5. Is Tokyo in China or Japan? (Yes, it is.   It is in Japan.   It is the capital.)

6. Why are you tired?
   (I am tired because I am sick.   I am in bed because I am tired.)

7. How old is your father? (He is a businessman.   He is fine.   He is 58.)

8. Is it cold in Canada in winter? (It is in the winter.   Yes, it is.)

9. Do you have a dictionary? (It is $50.   It is 2:00.   No.)

10. Which is more expensive—a car or a bicycle?
    (Yes, it is.   It is expensive.   A car is more expensive.)

11. How much is your rent? (It is $500 a month.   Yes, it is.)

12. What color is your hair? (No, it isn't.   It is black.   It is in the morning.)

Exercise 2: Dictation

Listen to your teacher. Complete the question. Then write the answer. Discuss the answers.

1. Question: _____ are you today?

   Answer: I'm _____.

2. Question: _____ is your name?

   Answer: My name is _____.

3. Question: Are _____ a _____?

   Answer: _____, I am.

4. Question: _____ is your teacher?

   Answer: My teacher is _____.

5. Question: _____ is your class?

   Answer: It is at _____.

6. Question: Are you _____ or _____?

   Answer: I am _____.

7. Question: _____ are you from?

   Answer: I am from _____.

8. Question: _____ are you in _____?

   Answer: I am here to study _____.

9. Question: _____ is your birthday?

   Answer: My birthday is _____.

10. Question: _____ you have a computer?

    Answer: _____.

Exercise 3

Read the answer. Then write the question word or words.

1. Question: _____<u>What time</u>_____ is the movie?
   Answer: The movie is at 6:00 p.m.

2. Question: _____ is the party?
   Answer: Tomorrow.

3. Question: _____ is he absent?
   Answer: Because he is sick.

4. Question: Is Antonio a man's name _____ a woman's name?
   Answer: A man's name.

5. Question: _____ is the Amazon River?
   Answer: In South America.

6. Question: _____ was the king of Jordan in the 1980s?
   Answer: King Hussein.

7. Question: _____ soccer popular in your country?
   Answer: Yes, it is.

8. Question: _____ are American dollars?
   Answer: Green.

9. Question: _____ you have a big home?
   Answer: No, I don't.

10. Question: _____ days are there in December?
    Answer: 31.

11. Question: _____ time is the first class?
    Answer: 8:00 a.m.

12. Question: _____ is bigger, an elephant or a mouse?
    Answer: An elephant.

Exercise 4

Write questions. Use the words given. Then write answers.

1. Who is

   Question: _Who is your friend?_

   Answer: _Abdullah._

2. What is

   Question: _____

   Answer: _____

3. Where is

   Question: _____

   Answer: _____

4. When is

   Question: _____

   Answer: _____

5. Why are

   Question: _____

   Answer: _____

6. Do you have

   Question: _____

   Answer: _____

7. How much is

   Question: _____

   Answer: _____

8. Are you / or

   Question: _____

   Answer: _____

1 *I, My, You, Your*

My homework is difficult!

I + Verb

Examples: I am a student. (or) I'm a student.
I speak English.

My + Noun

Examples: My father is a businessman.
Yasuko is my friend.

You + Verb

Examples: You are a good teacher.
You have a nice house.

Your + Noun

Examples: Your book is on the table.
What is your name?

Exercise 1: Dictation

Listen to your teacher. Complete the sentences.

1. _____ 'm _____ .

2. _____ first language is not _____ .

3. Where is _____ _____ ?

4. _____ are a _____ student.

Discuss

a. Are you hungry?
b. What languages do you speak?
c. Do you have a car? If yes, what kind?
d. How many students are in your class?

Exercise 2

Circle the correct words.

1. (I (My)) mother is a doctor.

2. What color is (you your) bike?

3. (I My) have a big family.

4. Do (you your) live in a city?

5. This is (I my) book, and that is (you your) book.

Discuss

a. Do you have a job? If yes, what is it?
b. Do you have a bike? If yes, what color is it?
c. Is your family big or small or medium-sized?
d. Do you like your town or city?

Exercise 3

Fix any mistakes.

1. ~~You~~ *Your* name is very long.

2. This is me brother.

3. Your are a good friend.

4. Black is my favorite color.

5. You teacher is very young.

6. My am cold.

Discuss

a. Do you have any sisters? If yes, how many?
b. What is your favorite color?
c. Is your classroom cold today?

Exercise 4

Fill in the blanks. Use each word. Use correct capital letters.

I	✔my	my	you	your

1. ____My____ eyes are brown.

2. _____ am tired.

3. Welcome to _____ home!

4. _____ are late.

5. What is _____ address?

Discuss

a. What color are your eyes?
b. Are you tired?
c. What time is your class?
d. Where do you live?

Exercise 5

Circle words to make questions. Complete the answers. Then discuss with a partner.

1. Question: What is (you   your) family name?

   Answer: _____ family name is _____ .

2. Question: What city are (you   your) from?

   Answer: _____ am from _____ .

3. Question: What is (you   your) father's job?

   Answer: _____ father is a _____ .

4. Question: What is (you   your) favorite food?

   Answer: _____ favorite food is _____ .

5. Question: What music do (you   your) like?

   Answer: _____ like _____ .

Exercise 6

Complete the sentences.

1. I am _____ .

2. Your home is _____ .

3. One of my friends is _____ .

4. My hair is _____ .

5. You are _____ .

Exercise 7

Complete the questions. Complete the answers. Then discuss with a partner.

1. Question: _____ is _____ name?

   Answer: _____ name is _____.

2. Question: _____ are _____ from?

   Answer: _____ 'm from _____.

3. Question: _____ is _____ birthday?

   Answer: _____ birthday is _____.

4. Question: Are _____ married or single?

   Answer: _____ am _____.

5. Question: Do _____ have any (brothers/sisters/children)?

   Answer: _____, _____ have

   _____.

6. Question: Why are _____ here?

   Answer: _____ am here to study English.

7. Question: Who is _____ teacher?

   Answer: _____ teacher is _____.

8. Question: _____ is _____ home now?

   Answer: _____ home is (in/at/on/near) _____.

9. Question: _____ is _____ favorite food?

   Answer: _____ favorite food is _____.

Subject Pronouns

My sister and I—We

Subject Pronouns

Singular	Plural
I	we
you	you
he	
she	they
it	

Meanings of Pronouns

Singular = one	**Plural = more than one**
I	we = you and I
you = one person	you = more than one person
he = Mr. Wilson	they = Mr. and Mrs. Kalfas
she = my sister	they = my books
it = my car	

Using Subject Pronouns

Examples: I am a student.
You are a good friend.
Mr. Wilson is a teacher. He is from Texas.
That is my sister. She is a student.
This is my car. It is very old.
You and I are classmates. We are also friends.
You (John and Pedro) are my best friends.
Mr. and Mrs. Kalfas are my neighbors. They are both Greek.
My books are at home. They are in my kitchen.

Exercise 1: Dictation

Listen to your teacher. Complete the sentences. Use correct capital letters.

1. _____ 'm ready for class. Are _____ ready?

2. The _____ is long, but _____ is good.

3. My cousin and _____ are together often.

   _____ are good friends.

4. _____ Selig is Canadian. _____ is from Toronto.

5. _____ Tran is not here today. Is _____ ill?

6. _____ are necessary, but _____ are expensive.

Discuss

a. How are you today?
b. What room are you and your classmates in?
c. Is your teacher Canadian?
d. How many pages does this book have?
e. Do you have cousins? Where do they live?
f. Do you have a computer? What kind is it?

Exercise 2

Write the names. Then write the subject pronouns.

1. ___Mona___ = ___she___
   (student)   (subject pronoun)

2. _____ = _____
   (student)   (subject pronoun)

3. _____ and _____ = _____
   (2 students)   (subject pronoun)

4. _____ = _____
   (something in the classroom) (subject pronoun)

5. _____ = _____
   (teacher)   (subject pronoun)

6. _____ and _____ = _____
   (something in the classroom) (something in the classroom) (subject pronoun)

7. _____ and I = _____
   (student)   (subject pronoun)

8. _____ = _____
   (your name)   (subject pronoun)

Exercise 3

Circle the correct words. Check punctuation and capital letters.

1. Claudia is smart, and (he (she) it) is friendly.

2. Jorge is not in class. (He   She   It) is absent (today   today.)

3. (Mr   Mr.) and Mrs. Singh are doctors. (He   She   They) are busy.

4. The apartment is expensive because (he   she   it) is (big.   small.)

5. (I   Me   My) daughter is in high school. (He   She   They) is 17 years old.

6. (you   You) and (I   my) are neighbors, and (we   they) are in the same class.

7. (Some   some) dogs are very small. (It   She   They) are often noisy.

Discuss

a. Who is absent today?
b. Do you have a sister? Is she a doctor?
c. Do you have children? How old are they?
d. Do you have a dog? What kind is it?

Exercise 4

Write a noun for each subject pronoun.

1. he: _my brother_
2. she: _____
3. it: _____
4. they: _____
5. we: _____
6. he: _____
7. they: _____
8. it: _____
9. we: _____

Exercise 5

Fix any mistakes.

1. Buenos Aires ~~it~~is in Argentina. ~~He~~ It is a big city.

2. Jakarta is a city. She is the capital of indonesia.

3. Spaghetti is a common Italian food. It is my favorite food.

4. my girlfriend she is 20 years old. Is a university student.

5. My husband and me are the same age. They are both 42 years old.

6. Mr. Carter he is good at tennis. she plays often.

7. Juan and Maria's first language is spanish. Are from Colombia.

Discuss

a. What is another big city? Where is it?
b. Do you like spaghetti? Is it your favorite food?
c. Do you have a favorite sport? What is it?
d. Do your friends play tennis?

Exercise 6

Circle words to make questions. Complete the answers.
Use subject pronouns.

1. Where is (you ⟨your⟩) father?

   _____ He _____ is __ in Taiwan _____ .

2. How old is (you your) mother?

   _____ is _____ .

3. What time is (you your) class finished?

   _____ is finished at _____ .

4. What color are (you your) eyes?

   _____ are _____ .

5. Is (you your) best friend here or in another country?

   _____ is _____ .

6. Are (you your) and (you your) classmates from the same country

   or from different countries?

   _____ are from _____ .

7. Is (you your) home now in a city, in a suburb, or in the country?

   _____ is _____ .

8. What city is (you your) teacher from?

   _____ is from _____ .

9. Are (you your) married or single?

   _____ am _____ .

Singular and Plural Nouns

Two men, one woman, three chairs, three glasses

Nouns with Regular Plurals

Singular (one)	Plural (more than one)
1 student	3 students
a tree	2 trees

Nouns with Irregular Plurals

Singular	Irregular Plural
1 child	4 children
a man	50 men
1 woman	a lot of women
1 person	20 people
1 knife	many knives

Plurals That Need -es

country—countries
bus—buses
dish—dishes
watch—watches
box—boxes

Adjective + Noun

a big house   two big houses
one good student   four good students

Exercise 1: Dictation

Listen to your teacher. Write the word that your teacher reads. Then
write the plural.

	Singular	Plural
1.	table	tables
2.		
3.		
4.		
5.		
6.		
7.		

Discuss

a. When does your family have parties?
b. How many days do you have class in one week?
c. How many women are there in your class?
d. Do you have any matches?

Exercise 2

Circle the correct words. Check punctuation.

1. Many people in the U.S. have three (name   names)—a first name,
   a middle name, and a last name.

2. New York and London are big (cities   citys).

3. There are 50 (state   states) in (the U.S.   the US,)

4. Theresa and Bob are (doctores   doctors).

5. There are many (old   olds) (house   houses) on my street.

6. The cost of this sandwich is (1$ $1), or one (dollar   dollars).

7. A dog has four (leg   legs) and a (tails   tail).

Discuss

a. How many names do you have?
b. What are the big cities in your home country?
c. What state do you live in? Have you lived in other states?
d. Are there many houses on your street?

Exercise 3

How many are in your classroom? Write the number and the noun.

1. wall: __4 walls__

2. desk: _____

3. teacher: _____

4. student: _____

5. window: _____

6. clock: _____

7. man: _____

8. woman: _____

9. child: _____

10. computer: _____

11. box: _____

Exercise 4

Fix any mistakes. Check for grammar and spelling.

1. There are three bedroom in the apartment.

2. Two familys live in the house.

3. How many childs do you have?

4. I have three littles sisteres.

5. Some peoples have cats.

6. There are knifes on the table.

7. We have dishes for 12 people.

8. Do we have 12 clean glass?

Discuss

a. How many bedrooms are there in your home?
b. Do you have any sisters?
c. Do you like cats? Do you have a cat?
d. How many animals do you have?

Exercise 5

Complete the sentences. Use correct punctuation.

1. I have three _____

2. There are two _____ in my home.

3. Do you have a _____

4. The Czech Republic and Slovakia are two different _____

5. In this city, there are many _____

6. People have 10 _____

Exercise 6

Answer "How many?" Use the words. Complete the sentences.

1. books in my backpack

    I have ___3 books in my backpack_____ .

2. people in my family

    There are _____ .

3. rooms in my home

    There are _____ .

4. cars

    My family has _____ .

5. letters in my first name

    There are _____ .

6. very good friends

    I have _____ .

7. days in this month

    There are _____ .

Exercise 7

Complete the sentences.

1. One minute has _____ seconds.

2. One hour has 60 _____ .

3. One day has 24 _____ .

4. There are seven _____ in a week.

5. There are four _____ in a month.

6. One year has 12_____ .

Adjectives

He is a rich man, but is he happy?

Examples of Adjectives

big
Canadian
cold
difficult
fast
happy
interesting
many
new
quiet
red
safe
sleepy
three
tired

Adjective + Noun

Examples: the red book
happy children
a big house
two big houses

Adjectives in Sentences

Examples: Russia is big.   (or)   Russia is a big country.
His shoes are new.   (or)   They are new shoes.
That book is interesting.   (or)   It is an interesting book.

Adjectives in Questions

Examples: Is the water cold?
No, it is not cold.

Are you sleepy?
Yes, I am sleepy.

Exercise 1: Dictation

Listen to your teacher. Write the words.

1. _____

2. _____

3. _____

4. _____

5. _____

Discuss

a. Are your shoes new or old?
b. Do you like green tea or black tea?
c. What is an expensive car?
d. Is English easy or difficult for you?

Exercise 2

Circle the correct words.

1. (He   His) is a (singer good   good singer).

2. Sometimes (Mexican food   food Mexican) (is spicy   spicy is).

3. Switzerland has (tall   talls) (mountain   mountains).

4. There are some (sick babys   sick babies) in the hospital.

5. My neighbors (quiet   are quiets   are quiet).

Discuss
a. Are you a good singer? Who is a good singer?
b. Do you like spicy food or mild food?
c. Are there tall mountains in your home country?
d. Is there a large hospital near your home?
e. Are your neighbors quiet or noisy?

Exercise 3

Fix any mistakes.

1. *Titanic* is a movie long.

2. Paris beautiful.

3. China and Egypt are olds countries.

4. Mr. Evans is a tall.

5. Is the class boring?

6. Elephants are not smalls.

Discuss
a. What is another long movie?
b. What is another beautiful city?
c. What is another old country?
d. How tall are you?
e. What is another big animal?

Exercise 4

Use the words. Make sentences.

1. a / city. / Bangkok / noisy / is

   Bangkok is a noisy city.

2. coffee / strong. / Turkish / very / is

   _____

3. My / busy. / and mother / are / father

   _____

4. in / is / cold / winter. / Germany

   _____

5. afraid of / are / children / dogs. / big / Some

   _____

Discuss

a. Is your city or town noisy or quiet?
b. Do you like strong coffee?
c. Are you busy today?
d. Is winter cold in your home country?
e. Are you afraid of anything? If yes, what are you afraid of?

Exercise 5

Fill in each blank. Use an adjective or a noun.

1. My mother is a/an _____ woman.

2. The U.S. is a/an _____ country.

3. Soccer is an exciting _____ .

4. Tokyo is a/an _____ .

5. A/An _____ is an expensive _____ .

6. _____ are interesting.

7. I have a/an _____ family.

Exercise 6

Circle words to make questions. Write answers.

1. Are (you   your) from a big country, a small country, or a medium-sized country?

   _____ am _____.

2. Is (you   your) best friend male or female?

   _____ is _____.

3. Are (you   your) sick or well today?

   _____ am _____.

4. Is (you   your) watch old or new?

   _____ is _____.

5. Is (you   your) teacher tall, short, or medium-sized?

   _____ is _____.

6. Are (you   your) neighbors friendly or unfriendly?

   _____ are _____.

Exercise 7

Complete the sentences. Use adjectives.

1. My chair is _____.

2. Summer is _____.

3. Apples are _____.

4. The weather today is _____.

5. A rabbit is _____.

6. My eyes are _____.

7. The library is _____.

8. Some students in our class are _____.

5 Demonstratives
This, That, These, Those

These pants are too big!

Meaning

this = singular—near speaker, here
that = singular—away from speaker, there
these = plural—near speaker, here
those = plural—away from speaker, there
Examples: This is my friend, Donaldo.
          This street is noisy.
          That is my teacher over there.
          That car is fast!
          These are my children.
          These sentences are difficult.
          Those are new.
          Those mountains are beautiful!

Exercise 1

Look at each picture. Write the correct demonstratives.

1. _____ building

2. _____ flowers

3. _____ door

4. _____ bus stop

5. _____ bus

6. _____ mountains

7. _____ clouds

8. _____ birds

9. _____ tree

10. _____ room

11. _____ photographs

12. _____ car

Exercise 2: Dictation

Listen to your teacher. Complete the sentences.

1. _____ is _____ .

2. _____ are _____ .

3. _____ are _____ .

4. _____ is _____ .

5. _____ is _____ .

Discuss

a. Do you have a pencil or a pen? Which one is yours?
b. Which book is yours?
c. Do you have a coin? If yes, what is it?
d. How many windows are there in this classroom? Are they open or closed?
e. Are the desks in this classroom old or new?

Exercise 3

Circle the correct words.

1. (This   That) restaurant is far away.

2. (This   These) soup (hot   is hot).

3. (These   Those) stores over there are (open   opens).

4. Is (that   those) (you   your) coat?

5. Shelley: Phil, (this   these   that   those) are (I   my) parents.
   Phil: Nice to meet (you   your).

Discuss

a. What restaurant do you like? Is that restaurant expensive?
b. What stores do you like? Are those stores near your house?
c. Do you have a coat? If yes, which coat is yours?
d. How do you introduce your teacher?
e. How do you introduce your friends?

Exercise 4

Fix any mistakes.

1. This two suitcase are heavy.

2. This woman over there is a doctor.

3. Those chairs are comfortable.

4. These CDs are expensives.

5. That guys across the street are very tall. They are basketball player.

Discuss

a. What is something heavy?
b. What is something light?
c. Are there chairs in your classroom? Are they comfortable?
d. Are there any tall people in your class?
e. Do you have any CDs? If yes, which CD is your favorite?

Exercise 5

Make sentences. Put the words in order.

1. this / book? / Is / your

   Is this your book?

2. that / your / Is / car?

   _____

3. my / These / are / sunglasses.

   _____

4. interesting. / This / is / magazine

   _____

5. your / those / over there? / Are / children

   _____

Exercise 6

Draw a simple picture of your family. Introduce your family to a partner. Then write sentences about your picture. Use *This, These, That,* or *Those.* Read the examples.

1. <u>This is my sister, Fernanda.</u>
2. <u>These are my boys, Eduardo and Miguel.</u>
3. _____
4. _____
5. _____
6. _____
7. _____
8. _____
9. _____

Exercise 7

Complete the sentences.

1. This _____ is big.
2. That boy is _____.
3. These _____ are old.
4. Those people over there are _____.
5. Is this your _____?
6. That _____ is very strong.
7. Are these your _____?
8. Those _____ over there are happy.

The Verb *Be*

6

These pyramids are in Egypt.

Forms of *Be*

Affirmative	Contractions
I am	I'm
you (singular) are	you're
he is	he's
she is	she's
it is	it's
we are	we're
you (plural) are	you're
they are	they're

Examples:

I am a good swimmer.	(or)	I'm a good swimmer.
You are right.	(or)	You're right.
She is from Hong Kong.	(or)	She's from Hong Kong.
It is a beautiful city.	(or)	It's a beautiful city.
We are classmates.	(or)	We're classmates.
They are English books.	(or)	They're English books.

Exercise 1: Dictation

Listen to your teacher. Write the sentences.

1. _____
2. _____
3. _____
4. _____
5. _____
6. _____

Discuss

a. What is the money of your home country? What color is it?
b. Are you ever late to class?
c. Is your best friend in this city now?

Exercise 2

Change the verbs to contractions. Write the sentences.

1. It is warm today.

   It's warm today.

2. I am on time every day.

   _____

3. You are a nice person.

   _____

4. She is a hard worker.

   _____

5. We are lucky.

   _____

6. They are from Cyprus.

   _____

Exercise 3

Circle the correct words.

1. (I tired   I'm tired   Tired I'm) today.

2. (I   Me   My) grandfather and (I   me   my) (am   is   are) close.

3. My mother (am   is   are) a (cook good   good cook).

4. Many (dentist   dentists) (am   is   are) (woman   women   womans).

5. The desert (hot   is hot   it is hot) in the summer.

Discuss

a. Are you tired today?
b. Is your grandfather alive? Are you and he close?
c. Is your mother a good cook? Are you a good cook?
d. Is your dentist a man or a woman?
e. In your home country, is there a desert?

Exercise 4

Fix any mistakes.

1. You're busy today.

2. My father 50 year old.

3. Flowers is pretty.

4. In winter, is cold in Korea

5. In Tokyo, apartments smalls.

6. She a friendly persons.

Discuss

a. How old are your parents?
b. What is an example of a flower?
c. Is it cold in your state in winter?
d. Where is Tokyo?

Exercise 5

Complete the questions. Use the verb *be*. Write answers. Discuss with a partner.

1. What color _____*are*_____ most soccer balls?
   (be)

   Most soccer balls are white and black.

2. What _____ your mother's name?
   (be)

   _____

3. Where _____ you from?
   (be)

   _____

4. What time _____ it now?
   (be)

   _____

5. Who _____ the leader of your home country?
   (be)

   _____

6. _____ your street safe or dangerous?
   (be)

   _____

Exercise 6

Complete the sentences. Use the correct form of the verb *be*.

1. My teacher _____.

2. I _____.

3. We _____.

4. Today, it _____.

5. They _____.

6. English _____.

7. My neighbors and I _____.

8. Today, my clothes _____.

Negative of the Verb *Be*

A turtle is not fast. It's slow.

Verb *Be*

Affirmative	Negative	Contractions		
I am	I am not	I'm not		
you are	you are not	you're not	(or)	you aren't
he is	he is not	he's not	(or)	he isn't
she is	she is not	she's not	(or)	she isn't
it is	it is not	it's not	(or)	it isn't
we are	we are not	we're not	(or)	we aren't
you are	you are not	you're not	(or)	you aren't
they are	they are not	they're not	(or)	they aren't

Exercise 1: Dictation

Listen to your teacher. Write the sentences.

1. _____

2. _____

3. _____

4. _____

5. _____

Discuss

   a. Are you and the teacher from the same country?
   b. What day is it today?
   c. How much is this book? Are you sure?
   d. How many students are in this class? Are they all here today?

Exercise 2

Change the verbs to contractions. Write the sentences.

1. English is not difficult. It is fun.

   English isn't difficult. It's fun.

2. I am not from here.

   _____

3. You are not the teacher.

   _____

4. She is not a nurse. She is a doctor.

   _____

5. We are not ready yet.

   _____

6. The dishes are not dirty. They are clean.

   _____

Exercise 3

Circle the correct words.

1. Rio de Janeiro (am   is   are) (no   not) the capital of Brazil.

2. Whales (not   isn't   aren't) fish. (It's   They're   He's) mammals.

3. The air in Mexico City (no is   not   is not   are not) clean.

4. Eggs (not expensive   is not expensive   are not expensive) in
   (me   my   I) supermarket. (It   He   They) (is   are) (cheap   cheaps).

5. Mount Everest (not   are not   is not) in China. (She's   It's   They're)
   in Nepal.

> ### Discuss
> a. What is the capital of Brazil? Are you sure?
> b. What is another mammal? What is one kind of fish?
> c. Is the air in your city clean?
> d. Do you like eggs? Are they expensive?
> e. What is another tall mountain? Are there mountains near your city?

Exercise 4

Fix any mistakes.

1. *Titanic* no is a new movie.

2. Rome and Florence not in England

3. We're not engineer.

4. Some people they not friendly.

5. I am thirsty, but I no am hungry.

> ### Discuss
> a. Is *Titanic* a good movie?
> b. Where are Rome and Florence?
> c. Are you an engineer? Is anyone in your family an engineer?
> d. Are you hungry now? Are you thirsty?

Exercise 5

Fill in each blank. Use a form of the verb be.

1. Elephants _____are_____ large. Ants _____are not_____ large.

2. Apples _____ vegetables. They _____ fruit.

3. Masako _____ an English name. _____ Japanese.

4. New York _____ the capital of the U.S. Washington, D.C.,

   _____ the capital.

5. I _____ from Europe. I _____ from

   _____ .

6. It _____ hot today. This room _____ cold.

Exercise 6

**Complete each question. Use the verb be. Write answers. Discuss
with a partner.**

1. _____Are_____ you a teacher?
   (be)
   __No, I'm not a teacher. I'm a student._____

2. _____ you 16 years old?
   (be)
   _____

3. _____ this an English class?
   (be)
   _____

4. _____ your books on the floor?
   (be)
   _____

5. _____ your best friend a student?
   (be)
   _____

6. _____ your grandparents from Europe?
   (be)
   _____

Exercise 7

Write true sentences. Use the words below the line. Use the verb *be*.

1. _Computers are not cheap._
    (computers / cheap)

    They're expensive.
    (expensive)

2. _____
    (bananas / blue)

    _____
    (yellow)

3. _____
    (I / happy / today)

    _____
    (I / unhappy)

4. _____
    (Switzerland / a poor country)

    _____
    (rich)

5. _____
    (baseball / popular in China)

    _____
    (popular / in the United States)

6. _____
    (my family / big)

    _____
    (small)

7. _____
    (my classmates / noisy)

    _____
    (quiet)

Discuss

a. Do you like bananas? Are they your favorite fruit?
b. What sports are popular in your home country?
c. Do you have a big family? How many people are in your family?
d. Are you a quiet person?

Exercise 8

Write true sentences. Use the words below the line. Use the verb *be*.

1. __My name isn't Elvis.__
(my name / not)

   __It is Jorge.__
(it)

2. _____
(summer in my home country / not)

   _____
(it)

3. _____
(my father / not)

   _____
(he)

4. _____
(people in my home country / not)

   _____
(they)

5. _____
(I / not)

   _____
(I)

6. _____
(Americans / not)

   _____
(they)

7. _____
(my teacher / not)

   _____
(he / she)

8. _____
(you / not)

   _____
(you)

9. _____
(my eyes / not)

   _____
(they)

Discuss

a. Is summer here like summer in your home country or state?
   How is it the same or different?
b. Are people here like people in your home country or state?
   How are they the same or different?

Prepositions of Time
In, At, On

The city is dark and quiet at 4:00 in the morning.

Time Expressions with Prepositions

times:	at 9:00, at 4:30 p.m., at noon, at midnight
days:	on Sunday, on Wednesdays, on the weekend
dates:	on December 31; on April 20, 1982
holidays:	on Christmas, on Thanksgiving
periods of the day:	in the morning, in the afternoon, in the evening, at night
months:	in February, in September
years:	in 2004, in 1982
seasons:	in summer, in spring
	(or)
	in the summer, in the spring

Time Expressions with No Prepositions

now, every day, today

Exercise 1: Dictation

Listen to your teacher. Write the time expressions.

1. _in the evening_ _____
2. _____
3. _____
4. _____
5. _____
6. _____
7. _____
8. _____

Exercise 2

Circle the correct words.

1. The game (no is   is not) (today   in today). (He's   It's)
    (in   on) the weekend.

2. (In   At   On) Sunday morning, the streets (not crowded   are not crowded).

3. January 1 (is   are) a holiday in many (country   countries).

4. There are no classes (in   at   on) New Year's Day.

5. Florida (is   it is   are) very hot (in   at   on) summer.

6. The test is (in   at   on) 11:00 (tomorrow   on tomorrow).

> ### Discuss
> a. When do you watch TV?
> b. When are the streets crowded?
> c. When are most stores closed?
> d. Is January 1 a holiday in your home country?
> e. What is the next holiday? When is it?

Exercise 3

Fix any mistakes.

1. There are a lot of party in the weekend.

2. Class is in 9:00 on Monday, Wednesday, and Friday.

3. His job is difficult. He is very tired in the night.

4. Terry's birthday is on May.

5. In some countries, skiing is popular in winter.

Discuss

a. What do you like to do on weekends?
b. When do you have classes?
c. Do you have a job? If yes, when do you work?
d. When is your birthday?
e. Do you ski? If yes, when?

Exercise 4

**Complete each question. Use the verb *be*. Write answers. Discuss
with a partner.**

1. What time _____ you finished with class today?
   (be)

   _____

2. _____ the bank open on Sundays?
   (be)

   _____

3. What time _____ dinner in your home?
   (be)

   _____

4. _____ you usually tired in the morning?
   (be)

   _____

5. In what month _____ there a big holiday in your home country?
   (be)

   _____

Exercise 5

Use the words. Make sentences. Add words and make changes as necessary.

1. many beach / be crowded / summer

   <u>Many beaches are crowded in summer.</u>

2. most people / be asleep / 2:00 a.m.

   _____

3. in many country / schools / be closed / December 25

   _____

4. Valentine's Day / be / February

   _____

5. some city / be not safe / night

   _____

Discuss

a. Do you ever go to the beach? If yes, when?
b. Are you usually asleep at 2:00 a.m.?
c. When are schools usually closed?

Exercise 6

Complete the sentences. Use time expressions.

1. Christmas Day is <u>on December 25</u>_____.

2. In my home country, the weather is nice _____.

3. On weekdays, I usually go to bed _____.

4. My home country's Independence Day is _____.

5. I shop for food _____.

6. The malls are busy _____.

7. In my home country, the school year starts _____.

8. There is a good TV program _____.

Yes/No and Or Questions with the Verb Be

Is Mount Everest in China?
No, it isn't. It's in Nepal.

Yes/No Questions and Answers

Examples: Are you a student?
Yes, I am.

Is she sick?
No, she isn't. She's fine.

Is the book in Spanish?
No, it isn't. It is in English.

Short Answers—Yes

Yes, I am.	Yes, we are.
Yes, you are.	Yes, you are.
Yes, he/she/it is.	Yes, they are.

Short Answers—*No*

No, I am not.	(or)	No, I'm not.	
No, you are not.	(or)	No, you're not.	(or) No, you aren't.
No, he is not.	(or)	No, she's not.	(or) No, it isn't.
No, we are not.	(or)	No, we're not.	(or) No, we aren't.
No, they are not.	(or)	No, they're not.	(or) No, they aren't.

Or Questions and Answers

Examples: Is your car red or black?

It's red.

Are your classes in the morning or the evening?
They're in the evening.

Exercise 1: Dictation

Listen to your teacher. Write the questions. Write answers. Discuss with a partner.

1. Question: _____

   Answer: _____

2. Question: _____

   Answer: _____

3. Question: _____

   Answer: _____

4. Question: _____

   Answer: _____

5. Question: _____

   Answer: _____

6. Question: _____

   Answer: _____

Exercise 2

Circle the correct words.

1. Question: (English is   Is English) your first language?
   Answer: No, (it is   it isn't).

2. Question: (Is   Are) Bonn and Berlin big (city   cities)?
   Answer: Yes, (they're   they are).

3. Question: (Houses are   Are houses) (in   at   on) this city
   cheap (and   or) expensive?
   Answer: (Yes, they are.   They are expensive.)

Exercise 3

Write questions about your classmates, family, friends, or famous people. Use the verb *be*. Then write the answers.

1. Question: _Are your parents_ _____ from Guatemala?

   Answer: _No, they aren't. They're from Costa Rica._ _____

2. Question: _____ from Mexico?

   Answer: _____

3. Question: _____ and _____ married?

   Answer: _____

4. Question: _____ in class or absent today?

   Answer: _____

5. Question: _____ a good actor?

   Answer: _____

Discuss

a. Are there students from Mexico in your class?
b. Are any students in your class married? If yes, who?
c. Is anyone absent today?
d. Who is a good actor?

Exercise 4

Use the words and the verb *be*. Write questions. Then write answers.

1. it / hot today?

   Question: _Is it hot today?_

   Answer: _No, it isn't. It's cool._

   it / cloudy / sunny?

   Question: _Is it cloudy or sunny?_

   Answer: _It's cloudy._

2. pizza / German food?

   Question: _____

   Answer: _____

3. jets / fast?

   Question: _____

   Answer: _____

4. the Nile River / in Africa / Asia?

   Question: _____

   Answer: _____

   you / sure?

   Question: _____

   Answer: _____

5. Barcelona / the capital of Spain?

   Question: _____

   Answer: _____

6. strawberries / a summer fruit / a winter fruit?

   Question: _____

   Answer: _____

Exercise 5

Use the words and the verb *be*. Write questions. Write the answers. Then discuss with a partner.

1. your car

   Question: _Is your car red?_

   Answer: _No, it isn't. It is blue._

2. your computer

   Question: _Is your computer new or old?_

   Answer: _It is new._

3. your eyes

   Question: _____

   Answer: _____

4. your favorite sport

   Question: _____

   Answer: _____

5. your favorite food

   Question: _____

   Answer: _____

6. your work

   Question: _____

   Answer: _____

7. your neighbors

   Question: _____

   Answer: _____

Wh- Questions with the Verb *Be*

Where are my keys?

Question Words

who
what
which
where
when
why
how
what time
what color
how many
how much
how long

Wh- Questions with the Verb *Be*

Examples: Where's the party? It's at my house.
What time is the meeting? It's at 9:00.
Who is he? He is my English teacher.
When is your class? It's on Mondays and Wednesdays.
Which notebook is yours? The blue notebook is mine.
How much is this ring? It's $299.
Why is Ramiro at home? He's at home because he's sick.
How many people are in your family? Seven.
How long is the movie? Two hours.

Exercise 1: Dictation

Listen to your teacher. Write the questions. Then write answers.

1. Question: _____

   Answer: _____

2. Question: _____

   Answer: _____

3. Question: _____

   Answer: There _____ .

4. Question: _____ Valentine's _____?

   Answer: _____

5. Question: _____ favorite?

   Answer: _____

Discuss

a. What is another city in China?
b. What is another holiday? When is it?
c. Do you have a favorite song? What is it?

Exercise 2

Circle words to make questions. Then write answers.

1. Question: (When   What) (is   are) (you   your) telephone number?

   Answer: _____

2. Question: (Where   When) (you are   are you) now?

   Answer: _____

3. Question: What time (it is   is it) now?

   Answer: _____

4. Question: How many (player   players) (is   are) there on a basketball team?

   Answer: There _____

Discuss
a. When is this class finished?
b. What are your favorite sports?

Exercise 3

Fix any mistakes. Answer the questions. Discuss with a partner.

1. Question: Where your teacher is from?

   Answer: _____

2. Question: How long is your class?

   Answer: _____

3. Question: Why you are tired?

   Answer: _____

4. Question: When are your birthday?

   Answer: _____

5. Question: Who are the person next to you?

   Answer: _____

Exercise 4

Complete each question. Write the answer.

1. Question: Who _____ the president of the U.S.?
   (be)

   Answer: _____

2. Question: Where _____ Caracas—in Venezuela or Peru?
   (be)

   Answer: _____

3. Question: What countries _____ near your home country?
   (be)

   Answer: _____

4. Question: Who _____ two famous people in your home country?
   (be)

   Answer: _____

Exercise 5

Read each answer. Complete the question.

1. Question: What _time is the meeting_____?

   Answer: The meeting is at 2:00 p.m.

2. Question: Which _____?

   Answer: That train is the express train.

3. Question: Why _____?

   Answer: He is happy because it is his birthday.

4. Question: When _____?

   Answer: The weekend in the United Arab Emirates is Thursday and Friday.

5. Question: Where _____?

   Answer: The Alps are in France and Italy.

Discuss

a. Are you happy today? If yes, why?
b. In your home country, when is the weekend?

Exercise 6

Complete each answer. Use the verb *be*. Then write the correct
Wh- question.

1. Question: ___Where is your teacher from?___

   Answer: My teacher _____is_____ from England.

2. Question: _____

   Answer: The bikes _____ in the garage.

3. Question: _____

   Answer: The rent _____ $500 a month.

4. Question: _____

   Answer: Those people _____ my classmates.

5. Question: _____

   Answer: The party _____ Saturday.

6. Question: _____

   Answer: There _____ 31 days in December.

7. Question: _____

   Answer: My hat _____ green.

8. Question: _____

   Answer: The room _____ hot because the fan is broken.

Discuss

a. Do you have a bike? Where is it?
b. How much is the rent for a small apartment in your city?
c. What month is it now? How many days are there in this month?
d. Is the classroom hot or cold today? Why?

Exercise 7

**Write questions. Use the words given and the verb *be*.
Then write answers.**

1. what street / your home on

   Question: _____

   Answer: _____

2. which city / your favorite

   Question: _____

   Answer: _____

3. how long / your classes

   Question: _____

   Answer: _____

Exercise 8

Write questions. Begin with the words given. Then write answers.

1. what color

   Question: _____

   Answer: _____

2. why

   Question: _____

   Answer: _____

3. where

   Question: _____

   Answer: _____

4. how many

   Question: _____

   Answer: _____

11 Count and Noncount Nouns
A/An, Some, Any

Some fruit in a bowl—an apple, some bananas, a pineapple, and some grapes, but not any peaches

Count Nouns

Examples: one girl
two miles
three houses

Noncount Nouns

Examples: fruit
music
tea

A/An + Singular Count Noun

Examples: a camera (one camera)
an apple (one apple)

Noncount Nouns: No *a/an*, No Plural

Examples: coffee
furniture
information
money
water

An + Word Beginning with *a, e, i, o, u*

Examples: an egg
an interesting book
Exception: a university

Some/Any + Plural Count Nouns

Examples: some books
some friends
any computers
any classes

Some/Any + Noncount Nouns (no plural)

Examples: some coffee
any time

Any with Questions and Negatives

Examples: Are there any computers in the room?
There aren't any computers in the room.

Is there any coffee in the pot?
There isn't any coffee in the pot.

Exercise 1: Dictation

Listen to your teacher. Write the sentences.

1. _____

2. _____

3. _____

4. _____

Exercise 2

Write the word *some* with each noun. Change the count nouns to plural. Do not change the noncount nouns.

1. car: _____ some cars
2. music: _____ some music
3. house: _____
4. ice: _____
5. information: _____
6. child: _____
7. meat: _____
8. sandwich: _____
9. woman: _____
10. penny: _____

Exercise 3

Circle the correct words.

1. London (is   are)   (big   a big) city.

2. Mr. Rodrigo has (office   a office   an office) in Madrid.

3. (A   Some) people (is not   are not) in class today.

4. There (is   are) (refrigerator   a refrigerator) in my apartment.

5. Are there any (holiday   holidays) this month?

6. Some (furniture   furnitures) (is   are) (expensive   expensives).

Discuss

a. Are you from a big city? Do you like big cities?
b. Do you have an office? If yes, where is it?
c. What is in your refrigerator now?
d. Is there a holiday this month? When is the next holiday?
e. What furniture do you have in your home?

Exercise 4

Fix any mistakes.

1. My brother is a smart.

2. A orange is a fruit.

3. There aren't any buses on that street.

4. Some big citys are not safes.

5. This is an important information.

6. Do you have a coffee?

Discuss

a. Do you have any brothers? If yes, are they smart?
b. Do you like fruit? If yes, what kinds of fruit do you like?
c. Are there many buses in your city?
d. What is a dangerous city? Is your city safe or dangerous?
e. Is grammar important?
f. Do you like coffee or tea?

Exercise 5

Fill in the blanks. Use the correct form of the words.

1. Japan _____ _____ .
   (be)   (island)

2. Brazil _____ _____ in South America.
   (be)   (country)

3. In some _____ , there _____ any
   (country)   (be not)
   _____ on Saturday.
   (class)

4. Do you have any _____ or _____ ?
   (rice)   (bread)

5. Some _____ _____ strict.
   (teacher)   (be not)

6. In some _____ , there _____ a lot of
   (bar)   (be)
   _____ .
   (smoke)

Exercise 6

Write sentences. Use correct forms of the words.
Add words when necessary.

1. Russian / be not / easy language

   _____

2. Christmas / be / big holiday in the West

   _____

3. this music / be / exciting

   _____

4. some store / be / busy / the weekend

   _____

5. there / be not / any lion / in the zoo

   _____

Discuss

a. Is Christmas a big holiday in your home country?
b. What kind of music do you like?
c. What stores in your city are busy on the weekend?
d. Is there a zoo in your city? Are there any lions in it?

Exercise 7

Complete the questions. Change or add words when necessary.
Then write answers.

1. What _____ some island _____?
              (be)   (country)

   _____

2. _____ easy language?
              (English / be)

   _____

3. _____ there any _____ in your classroom?
         (be)   (computer)

   _____

Exercise 8

Write sentences about these people.

1. My mother

   <u>My mother is an eye doctor.</u>

2. My father

   _____

3. My (brother/sister)

   _____

4. My mother

   _____

5. My (uncle/aunt)

   _____

6. I

   _____

Exercise 9

Complete the sentences. Put a noun or name in the first blank.

1. _____<u>Golf</u>_____ is a great _____<u>sport</u>_____ .

2. _____ is a happy _____ .

3. _____ is an interesting _____ .

4. Some _____ are _____ .

5. There are not any _____ in _____ .

6. A _____ is _____ .

7. Some _____ isn't _____ .

8. I don't have any _____ .

12 *There Is* and *There Are*

There are a lot of famous paintings in the museum.

There is + Singular Subject

Examples: There is a supermarket near my home.
There is a lot of information on the Internet.

There are + Plural Subject

Examples: There are three bikes in the garage.
There are some big stores on that street.

Contractions

Affirmative	**Negative**
There is = There's	There is not = There isn't
There are = There're	There are not = There aren't

Questions and Answers

Examples: Is there a zoo in your city? Yes, there is. (or) No, there isn't.
How many days are there in December? There are 31.

Negatives

Examples: There is no milk in the refrigerator.
There isn't any milk in the refrigerator.

There are no American students in our class.
There aren't any American students in our class.

Exercise 1: Dictation

Listen to your teacher. Write the sentences.

1. _____

2. _____

3. _____

4. _____

5. _____

6. _____

Discuss
a. Are there a lot of trains in your home country?
b. Is there a lot of traffic in your city or town? If yes, when?
c. Are there any stores near your home? If yes, which stores?

Exercise 2

Circle the answers.

1. (There   It) is (book   a book) on the table.

2. (Is   Are) there 30 or 31 (day   days) (in   on) November?

3. There (is   are) (a   the) (mall big   big mall) in the city.

4. There (isn't   aren't) (an   any) computers in that classroom.

5. (Who   How) much (money   moneys) (there is   is there) in the account?

Exercise 3

Fix any mistakes.

1. There is the sofa in my apartment.

2. There are a museum and an airport in my hometown.

3. Is there many freeway in Los Angeles?

4. There are not any mails in my mailbox today.

5. There is an old building on my street.

6. It is a new TV in Room 205.

Discuss

a. Do you have a sofa? If yes, where is it?
b. Is there a museum or an airport in your city?
c. Are there any freeways in your city?
d. Do you have a mailbox? If yes, where is it?
e. Is there a TV in your classroom?

Exercise 4

Write sentences. Change and add words when necessary.

1. there / be / a lot of immigrant / in the United States

   _____

2. there / be / no city / in Antarctica

   _____

3. there / be not / any ice / refrigerator

   _____

4. there / be not / any woman / on our football team

   _____

Exercise 5

Write questions. Use *how many* and *there is* or *there are*. Change words when necessary. Then write answers.

1. student / in your class?

    Question: How many students are there in your class?

    Answer: There are 18 students in our class.

2. telephone / in your classroom

    Question: _____

    Answer: _____

3. computer / in your classroom

    Question: _____

    Answer: _____

4. desk / in your classroom

    Question: _____

    Answer: _____

5. map / in your classroom

    Question: _____

    Answer: _____

6. man and woman / in your class

    Question: _____

    Answer: _____

7. student from your home country / in your class

    Question: _____

    Answer: _____

Exercise 6

**Write a sentence for each topic. Start with *There is* or *There are*.
Then discuss with a partner.**

1. babies in your family

   There is one baby in my family.

2. boys and girls in your family

   _____

3. a video store near your apartment or house

   _____

4. regions or states in your home country

   _____

5. factories in this city

   _____

6. a post office near your school

   _____

7. meat in your refrigerator right now

   _____

8. bedrooms in your home

   _____

9. an airport in your hometown

   _____

10. clouds in the sky today

    _____

11. gas in your car right now

    _____

Exercise 7

Write questions. Start with *Is there* or *Are there*. Add words when necessary. Then write short answers.

1. __Are there_____ many trains in the U.S.?

   __No, there aren't._____

2. _____ art museum in this city?

   _____

3. _____ bus stops on your street?

   _____

4. _____ ballpark near your home?

   _____

5. _____ much traffic in front of your school?

   _____

6. _____ pay phone near your classroom?

   _____

7. _____ movie theaters near your home?

   _____

8. _____ much furniture in your home?

   _____

9. _____ university in your hometown?

   _____

10. _____ Italian restaurant near your home?

    _____

Imperatives

**Hurry up, please, but be careful!
Don't drop the dishes.**

Imperatives

Examples: Listen. This is important.
Be quiet!
Turn off your cell phone.

Negative Imperative and Contraction

Examples: Do not sleep in class!
Don't be afraid. My dog is friendly.

Imperatives with *Please*

Examples: Sign your name, please.
Please close the door.

Exercise 1: Dictation

Listen to your teacher. Write the sentences.

1. _____

2. _____

3. _____

4. _____

5. _____

6. _____

7. _____

Discuss

a. Do you have your keys with you?
b. Do you speak English or your first language with your friends?
c. What do you do to get ready for class?
d. Who puts out the trash at your house?
e. Are the lights in this room turned on or off?

Exercise 2

Circle the correct words.

1. Please (not   no   don't) (eat   drink   be) too (much   many) soda.

2. (Make up   Put out   Turn off) the radio, please.

3. (No   Not   Do not) (give   have   like) him (a   any) money.

4. Please (don't angry   don't be angry   not angry).

5. (Write   Play   Watch) (you   your) name here, please.

6. (Not   Do not   No) drive over the speed limit.

Discuss

a. Do you like soda?
b. Do you listen to the radio in English?
c. What makes you angry?
d. How do you sign your name?
e. What is the speed limit on highways in your home country?

Exercise 3

Fill in the blanks. Use the verb _be_ in the first sentence. Then use a verb from the list. Write both sentences.

be	be	clean	close	eat	✔feed	go	help

1. Your dog _____**is**_____ (be) hungry. Please _____**feed**_____ (verb) him.

   __Your dog is hungry. Please feed him.__

2. It _____ (be) cold in here. Please _____ (verb) the window.

   _____

3. The baby _____ (be) asleep. Please _____ (verb) quiet.

   _____

4. You _____ (be) tired. Please _____ (verb) to bed.

   _____

5. That meat _____ (be) old. Do not _____ (verb) it.

   _____

6. The meeting _____ (be) at 7:00 a.m. Please don't _____ (verb) late.

   _____

7. The exercise _____ (be) difficult. Please _____ (verb) me.

   _____

8. The room _____ (be) dirty. Please _____ (verb) it.

   _____

Discuss

a. Is the classroom window open or closed?
b. Do you have a baby at home?
c. Are you tired today?
d. Do you like meat?
e. Do you like to clean?

Exercise 4

Read the first sentence. Then complete the imperative. Use a verb from the list. Use capital letters where you need to.

be careful	hurry up	slow down	turn on
don't forget	put	take off	write
don't talk	repeat	✔ turn down	

1. The radio is too loud.

   Please ___turn down_____ the volume.

2. It's hot.

   _____ your sweater.

3. We are late.

   _____!

4. You are in the library.

   Please _____ so loudly.

5. The room is very dark.

   _____ the light, please.

6. That sentence is difficult.

   Please _____ it.

7. This information is very important.

   _____ it!

8. There are a lot of police officers on this street.

   _____, please.

9. Here is your credit card.

   _____ your name on it, and _____ it in

   your wallet.

10. This new camera is very expensive.

    Please _____ with it!

Exercise 5

Write an imperative sentence to each person or group. Then discuss with a partner.

1. to your mother

   Mom, please write to me.

2. to your father or mother

   _____

3. to your best friend

   _____

4. to your teacher

   _____

5. to your classmates

   _____

6. to your brother or sister

   _____

7. to a child

   _____

8. to your neighbors

   _____

9. to the leader of your country

   _____

10. to a police officer

    _____

11. to the leaders of your city or town

    _____

Present Tense of Verbs

14

In China, people eat a lot of rice.

Present Tense

Singular Subject	**Plural Subject**
I speak.	We study.
You have. (one person)	You have. (more than one person)
He calls.	They need.
She walks.	
It starts.	

Forming the Present Tense

***I/you/we/they* + Verb**	***He/she/it* + Verb + *s***
I eat.	Yuming eats. (or) He eats.
You see.	Mrs. Flores sees. (or) She sees.
We open.	The store opens. (or) It opens.
They like.	

Spelling

have—has
do—does
go—goes
study—studies
watch—watches
brush—brushes
fix—fixes

Using the Present Tense

Examples: I speak English.
We study at the library.
You have a big house.
He watches TV on the weekend.
The movie starts at 7:30.
They need a new car.

Questions and Answers

Examples: Do you like spicy food? Yes, I do. (or) No, I don't.
Does she have a car? Yes, she does. (or) No, she doesn't.
Do we have a test today or tomorrow? We have a test today.
Where do they live? They live on River Road.

Exercise 1: Dictation

Listen to your teacher. Write the sentences.

1. _____
2. _____
3. _____
4. _____
5. _____

Discuss

a. How do you get to class? Do you take a bus?
b. Where do you do your homework?
c. Does it snow a lot in your city?

Exercise 2

Circle the correct words.

1. Many (African   Africans) (speak   speaks) two (language   languages).

2. The sun (come   comes) up in the east and (go   goes) down in the west.

3. (A   An) insect (have   has) six (leg   legs) and three body (part   parts).

4. (I   My) teacher (know   knows) English.

5. A lot of people in Beijing (ride   rides) (bicycle   bicycles).

> ### Discuss
> a. How many languages do you speak?
> b. What kind of weather do you like?
> c. What is an example of an insect?
> d. Does your teacher know another language?
> e. Do you have a bicycle? If yes, do you ride it much?

Exercise 3

Fix any mistakes.

1. These carrots come from California.

2. People in Mexico are eat lot of beans.

3. My father work for small company.

4. We listens to music from many different country.

5. I am like music a lot.

6. She have browns eyes.

> ### Discuss
> a. Do you like vegetables? What is your favorite vegetable?
> b. Do you eat a lot of beans?
> c. Where does your father work? Where do you work?
> d. What kind of music do you like?
> e. In your class, who has brown eyes?

Exercise 4

Fill in the blanks. Use the names of people you know. Then write a verb from the list. Use the correct form of the verb.

be	eat	have	speak	watch
drive	go	✔ play	study	wear

1. _____Claudia_____ _____plays_____ basketball on the weekend.
   (name)   (verb)

2. _____ _____ black hair.
   (name)   (verb)

3. _____ _____ to the movies often.
   (name)   (verb)

4. _____ and _____ _____ a lot
   (name)   (name)   (verb)
   of fast food.

5. _____ _____ English very well.
   (name)   (verb)

6. _____ and _____ _____
   (name)   (name)   (verb)
   to school.

7. _____ _____ TV every day.
   (name)   (verb)

8. _____ and _____ _____
   (name)   (name)   (verb)
   my friends.

9. _____ _____ glasses.
   (name)   (verb)

10. _____ _____ at the library.
   (name)   (verb)

Discuss

a. Do you have a favorite sport? Do you watch it or play it?
b. What do you do on the weekend?
c. Do you like fast food? How often do you eat it?
d. What languages do you speak well?
e. Do you wear glasses? If yes, when do you wear them?

Exercise 5

Circle verbs to make questions. Then write answers. Use the present tense.

1. Where do you (make   buy   live) groceries?

   _____

2. On weekdays, what time do you (go   have   sleep) to bed at night?

   _____

3. Do you (come   call   work) your friends often?

   _____

4. What kind of movies do you (read   close   like)?

   _____

5. What do you (swim   do   put) on weekends?

   _____

Exercise 6

Write sentences. Use the words given. Add and change words when necessary.

1. my house / have

   _____

2. my neighbor / go

   _____

3. many people / want

   _____

4. that woman / study

   _____

5. the child / brush

   _____

Present Tense Third Person Singular *-s*

He plays tennis every day.

He/she/it + Verb + s

Examples: I like sushi. He likes pizza.
You want pizza. Kelly wants tacos. (or) She wants tacos.
We drink soda. The dog drinks water. (or) It drinks water.

He/she/it + has

Examples: You have short hair.
My dad has no hair. (or) He has no hair.
We have black hair.
She has brown hair.
They have long hair.
The cat has fur. (or) It has fur.

Verbs that add -es

Examples: do—does
go—goes
push—pushes
watch—watches
fix—fixes
kiss—kisses
cry—cries
study—studies

Exercise 1: Dictation

Listen to your teacher. Write the sentences.

1. _____

2. _____

3. _____

4. _____

5. _____

Discuss

a. Where does the leader of your home country live?
b. Does it rain a lot in your city?
c. Do you have a car? If yes, what year is it?
d. What does *tiny* mean?
e. How long does it take you to go from your home to school?

Exercise 2

Circle the correct words.

1. A horse (run   runs) fast because its legs (is   are) (strong   strongs).

2. Every (morning   mornings), he (has   have) tea and toast for breakfast.

3. (Me   My) sister (like   likes) chicken, but I (like   likes) fish.

4. She (study   studies   studys) English (in   at   on) the evening.

5. He (watch   watchs   watches) the news before he (gos   goes) to work.

Exercise 3

Fix any mistakes.

1. At the summer, many people plays tennis.

2. My friend Pon eat rice almost every day.

3. Her brother is work in the night.

4. She clean her house in the weekend.

5. He cooks dinner for his family.

Discuss

a. What kinds of food do you eat often?
b. Does anyone in your family work at night? Who does?
c. When do you clean your house?

Exercise 4

Circle words to make questions. Then write answers.

1. What does (you   your) family do (at   on   in) Saturday?

   _____

2. How many (leg   legs) does (a   an) octopus have?

   _____

3. In (you   your) family, what do (person   people) like for dessert?

   _____

4. (Who   How) helps you (lot   a lot)?

   _____

5. What time does your mother get up (in   in the   at) morning?

   _____

6. (Who   Where) does your neighbor park his or her car?

   _____

Exercise 5

Fill in the blanks. Use the correct forms of the words.

1. My father _____ (be) 57 _____ (year) old, but he _____ (look) very young.

2. Mrs. Mendoza _____ (have) a car, but she _____ (walk) to work every day because her office _____ (be not) far.

3. In Montreal, Canada, most people _____ (speak) French, but my friend from Toronto, Canada, _____ (speak) only English.

4. Elena _____ (be) married. She _____ (have) two young _____ (child).

Discuss

a. Do you walk or drive to class?
b. Does anyone in your family speak two languages?
c. Is anyone in your class married? Does anyone have children?

Exercise 6

Complete the sentences. Use verbs from the list.

are	eats	has	is
eat	goes	have	snows

1. My dog _____ meat.

2. Cars _____ four wheels.

3. Los Angeles _____ a lot of freeways.

4. My father _____ to work at 8 a.m.

5. An apple _____ red.

6. Cows _____ grass.

7. Sao Paolo and Caracas _____ big cities.

8. It _____ in the winter.

Exercise 7

Fill in the blanks. Use the names of people you know. Use the correct form of the verbs.

1. _____ _____ short hair.
   (name)   (have)

2. _____ _____ glasses.
   (name)   (wear)

3. _____ _____ tall.
   (name)   (be)

4. _____ _____ coffee every day.
   (name)   (drink)

5. _____ and _____
   (name)   (name)
   _____ in the front of the classroom every day.
   (sit)

6. _____ _____ English outside of class.
   (name)   (speak)

7. _____ _____ very well.
   (name)   (dance)

Exercise 8

Fill in the blanks. Use be or other verbs. Use the present tense.

1. Ingrid _____ from Germany. She _____ blue eyes.

2. Marco _____ TV when he _____ dinner.

3. My brother _____ to the radio when he _____ his car.

4. Your sister _____ her homework in the library. _____ she a good student?

5. Every day, Inho _____ an e-mail to his girlfriend because he _____ her.

6. Susan _____ a shower before she _____ to bed.

Exercise 9

Write sentences. Use the words given. Add or change words when necessary. Use the present tense.

1. my mother / like

   _____

2. my friend / live

   _____

3. my teacher / bring

   _____

4. my classmates / know

   _____

5. my neighbor / have

   _____

6. cats / be

   _____

7. one student / carry

   _____

Exercise 10

What does your teacher do? Write sentences about your teacher.

1. Every day, _____.

2. In the morning, _____.

3. At night, _____.

4. On Friday night, _____.

5. On the weekend, _____.

16 Present Tense
Be and Other Verbs

They are young, but they play very well.

Verb Review: The Verb *Be*

Examples: Cairo is a big city.
Vegetables are good for you.
Oxford University is in England.
Their jobs are hard, but interesting.

Verb Review: Other Verbs

Examples: My friend dances a lot.
People in Brazil speak Portuguese.
She plays tennis very well.
The buses run all night.

Questions and Answers

Examples: Where is your office? It's downtown.
What time do you leave for work? I leave for work at 7:00 a.m.

Exercise 1: Dictation

Listen to your teacher. Write the sentences.

1. _____ Holland _____ .

2. _____ Taiwan _____ .

3. Cairo _____ Shanghai _____ .

4. _____ .

> ### Discuss
> a. Do many people in your home country speak English?
> b. What is another country that has warm winters?
> c. Where is Cairo? What country is Shanghai in?
> d. Are there mountains near your city?

Exercise 2

Circle the correct words.

1. Japan (is   are) a small country, but (it   he) (are   has) many people.

2. Many students (is   are   study) French and Spanish because French and Spanish (common   is common   are common) (language   languages).

3. (On   In) the summer, many people (is   are   go) to the beach because (is hot   hot   it is hot   are hot) in the cities.

4. A lot of (people   peoples) (have   are   come) cell phones, and (they   he) (are use   uses   use) the phones everywhere.

5. Shakespeare (is   speak   are   writes) a famous English writer. Many students (are   read   is   write) his plays.

6. Disneyland (is   are   visit) a popular place. Millions of people (is   are   visit   have) Disneyland every (year   years).

> ### Discuss
> a. Where do you go on vacation?
> b. Do you have a cell phone? If yes, do you use it a lot?
> c. What plays by Shakespeare do you know?
> d. Where is Disneyland?

Exercise 3

Fix any mistakes.

1. The canadian flag red and white.

2. My brother write with his left hand.

3. Horses runs fast.

4. Many countries has presidents.

5. Arabic not a language easy.

6. We are watch TV in night.

> **Discuss**
> a. What color is the flag of your home country?
> b. Do you write with your left hand or your right hand?
> c. Do you watch much TV? When do you watch TV?

Exercise 4

Circle words to make questions. Then write answers.
Write complete sentences.

1. What (is   are) your mother's name?

   _____

2. When do (you   your) buy groceries?

   _____

3. (How   Who) lives with you?

   _____

4. Where (is   are) your neighbors from?

   _____

5. Where do you (do   make) your homework?

   _____

Exercise 5

Complete the sentences. Use verbs from the list. Add subjects when necessary.

are	exercises	have	is	wears
are	goes	✔is	is not	work
drink	has	is	live	

1. When _____*it is*_____ cold, my son _____ warm clothes.

2. Both Tokyo and Paris _____ subways. _____ often crowded.

3. The leaders of the United States _____ the president and the Congress. _____ very hard.

4. Some people _____ a lot of alcohol, but too much alcohol _____ healthy.

5. The Queen of England _____ a famous ruler. She and her husband _____ in London.

6. On Fridays, Karl _____ dancing with his friends. _____ a good time.

7. Katrina _____ strong because she _____ at the gym every day.

Discuss

a. What do you wear in cold weather?
b. Does your city have a subway? Is it crowded?
c. Who is another famous ruler? Where does he or she live?
d. What do you do on Fridays?
e. Do you exercise? If yes, where do you exercise?

Exercise 6

Complete the sentences. Start with names of people you know. Then use the verb *be* or other verbs.

1. _____Susumu has_____ black hair.

2. _____ friendly people.

3. _____ very tall.

4. _____ blue jeans almost every day.

5. _____ a lot of coffee.

6. _____ friendly.

7. _____ hamburgers a lot.

Exercise 7

Write sentences. Use the words given. Add words when necessary.

1. I / hungry

   _____

2. people in the U.S. / like

   _____

3. we / read

   _____

4. my friend / go

   _____

5. your teacher / know?

   _____

6. she / go shopping

   _____

7. I / love

   _____

Prepositions of Place

He teaches at a school in New York.

Some Prepositions of Place

in
at
on
to
from
over/above
under/below
near
far from
next to
in front of
behind
between

Preposition + Noun or Noun Phrase or Pronoun

Examples: Panama is between Colombia and Costa Rica.
Sit next to him.

In

Examples: The newspaper is in the kitchen.
There are a lot of advertisements in the newspaper.

On

Examples: I live on Hill Street. My house is on the left.
There is news on the radio, on TV, and on the Internet.

At

Examples: The store is at 456 East First Street.
My roommate is not at home now. She is at school.

To/From

Examples: Come to the meeting. Then go to the movie.
He's from Nigeria.

Other Prepositions of Place

Examples: I sit next to Francisco.
The painting is over the sofa.
The teacher stands in front of the class.

No Preposition

Example: After work, he goes home.

Exercise 1: Dictation

Listen to your teacher. Write the sentences.

1. _____

2. _____

3. _____

4. _____

Look at each picture. Fill in the blanks. Use prepositions of place.

1. The woman is _____ work.

2. She sits _____ her desk.

3. There is a computer _____ the desk.

4. She keeps her pens _____ a cup.

5. Her desk is _____ the window.

6. A plant is _____ the cup of pens.

7. The fruit is _____ the bowl.

8. The bowl is _____ the table.

9. It is _____ the books and the mug.

10. The mug is _____ the right side.

11. The books are _____ the left side.

12. There are lights _____ the table.

13. The boy sits _____ his father.

14. They sit _____ a bench.

15. The bench is _____ a tree.

16. They have cones _____ their hands.

17. A car is _____ the store.

18. No one is _____ the car.

Exercise 3

Circle the correct words.

1. When people (goes go) (in on) vacation, (he they) often stay (at on to) a hotel.

2. (There is There are) a nice restaurant (next next to) our hotel.

3. (In At On To) many Mexican (city cities), people sell food (at on to) the streets.

4. (In every Every) summer, many people (go goes) (in at on to) the mountains.

5. On vacation, we (sit sits) (on in to) the beach and swim (in at on to) the ocean.

6. (I I'm) tired. Let's go (in home to home home).

Discuss

a. Where do you go on vacation?
b. Do people sell food on the streets in the U.S.? Where do they sell it?
c. Are there mountains in your home country?
d. Where do you like to swim?
e. Is there a beach near your home? How far is it?

Exercise 4

Fix any mistakes.

1. Young childrens usually go in bed before 9:00 p.m.

2. My friends are at a party now.

3. The TV on the living room is new or old?

4. The president of egypt lives to Cairo.

5. In soccer, a goalie stand front of the goal.

6. They live in 1276 Main Street.

7. My dog sleep on the floor in the night.

Exercise 5

Answer the questions. Write complete sentences. Use prepositions.

1. Where are your (parents/children) now?

   _____

2. Do you usually eat dinner at home or in a restaurant?

   _____

3. Where are your books?

   _____

4. Where do you shop for food?

   _____

Exercise 6

Write sentences. Use the words given. Change and add words when necessary.

1. she / have / cell phone / her purse

   _____

2. there / be / any computer / library?

   _____

3. we live / apartment / Rose Street

   _____

4. every day / he / read / news from his country / the Internet

   _____

Discuss
a. Do you have a cell phone? If yes, where is it now?
b. Is there a library near your home? Where is it?
c. Do you live in an apartment or a house? What is it near?
d. Where do you read, see, or hear the news?

Exercise 7

Write complete answers. Use prepositions.

1. Where is Iran—next to Pakistan or next to India?

   _____

2. What country is between Finland and Norway?

   _____

3. What country is next to Spain?

   _____

4. What country is above the United States on the map?

   _____

5. What country is Addis Ababa in?

   _____

6. What countries are near El Salvador?

   _____

7. Where is your home country?

   _____

Exercise 8

Write about your class. Use student names or the word *nobody*.

1. _____ is next to _____.

2. _____ is between _____ and

   _____.

3. _____ is behind _____.

4. _____ and _____ are on the left side of the class.

5. _____ is in the front row.

6. _____ and _____ are in the back of the room.

7. _____ is near the door.

Exercise 9

Fill in the blanks. Use the names of people, places, or things. Add words as necessary.

1. _____The United Nations_____ is in _____New York_____.
   (place)   (city)

2. _____ is in _____.
   (city)   (country)

3. _____ is at _____.
   (person)   (place)

4. _____ often goes to _____.
   (person)   (store)

5. _____ is in _____.
   (thing)   (room)

6. _____ is near _____.
   (town)   (city)

7. _____ is in front of _____.
   (thing)   (building)

Exercise 10

Write sentences about places in your town or city.
Use the words given.

1. on

   _____The bank is on Main Street._____

2. near

   _____

3. far from

   _____

4. on

   _____

5. next to

   _____

6. behind

   _____

Adverbs of Frequency

He is usually on time because he always wears a watch.

Adverbs of Frequency

always
usually
often
sometimes
seldom
rarely
never

Verb *Be* + Adverb of Frequency

Examples: I am sometimes late for class.
He is often quiet.

Questions with the Verb *Be*

Example: Are you usually on time for class?

Adverb of Frequency + Other Verbs

Examples: He rarely cooks.
We never eat in class.

Sometimes, Often, and Usually at the Beginning of a Sentence

Examples: Sometimes I watch baseball on TV.
Usually it is cold in the winter.

Questions with How often . . .?

Example: How often do you watch TV? I seldom watch TV.

Exercise 1

Add adverbs of frequency to write true sentences. Discuss with a partner.

1. I read the newspaper in the morning.

   I usually read the newspaper in the morning.

2. I smoke.

   _____

3. I dance at parties.

   _____

4. People in my city are friendly.

   _____

5. I dream in English.

   _____

6. My parents send e-mail to me.

   _____

7. I drive fast.

   _____

Exercise 2

Circle the correct words. Make true sentences.

1. Winter in Alaska is (**always** often never) cold.

2. Summer (in at on) Mexico (is are) (always usually never) cold.

3. It (always usually rarely) (rain rains are rain) in the desert.

4. Doctors (in at on) the U.S. (usually seldom never) work hard.

5. (Children Childrens) (always sometimes never) tell lies.

6. My teacher is (always usually sometimes rarely never) late.

Exercise 3

Write sentences. Put the words in the correct order.
Check punctuation.

1. neighbor / noisy / my / is / sometimes

   _____

2. coffee / always / in the / drink / morning / I

   _____

3. rarely / dinner / her husband / cooks

   _____

4. beaches / in / are / usually / the summer? / crowded

   _____

5. loud / listen to / people / music / often / young

   _____

Discuss

a. Are your neighbors usually noisy or quiet?
b. What do you drink in the morning?
c. Who usually cooks dinner in your family? Who rarely cooks?
d. How often do you go to the beach?
e. What kinds of music do you listen to?

Exercise 4

Complete the sentences. Use the adverbs given. Add the verb *be* or other verbs.

1. They _____never watch_____ TV at night because they _____are always_____ tired.
   (never)   (always)

2. He _____ breakfast because he _____ late
        (rarely)   (always)
   for work.

3. She _____ tired at night because she _____ a
         (sometimes)   (always)
   lot of homework.

4. I _____ to bed before midnight, but I _____ up
       (usually)   (seldom)
   before 6:00 a.m.

5. I _____ angry because my friends _____
       (sometimes)   (never)
   English to me.

Discuss
a. Do you usually eat breakfast? What do you like for breakfast?
b. Are you usually tired after class? If yes, why?
c. What time do you go to bed? What time do you get up?
d. Do you speak English to your friends?

Exercise 5

Fix any mistakes.

1. It always cold in winter in Moscow.

2. Dogs often sleeps at the afternoon.

3. Never my father is sick because is a man strong.

4. Abdullah plays sometimes soccer in Saturdays.

5. My friend drinks rarely beer, but he loves soda.

Exercise 6: Dictation

Listen to your teacher. Write the sentences. Decide if each sentence is true (T) or false (F). If false, make the sentence true.

1. _It is never hot in the Sahara Desert in the summer._
   F—It is always hot in the Sahara Desert in the summer.

2. _____

3. _____

4. _____

5. _____

Exercise 7

Complete the sentences. Start with the names of classmates. Use the words given. Add the verb *be* or other verbs.

1. ____Ella____ ____is often____ late.
   (name)   (often)

2. _____ _____ on time for class.
   (name)   (always)

3. _____ and _____ _____
   (name)   (name)   (rarely)
   their first language in class.

4. _____ _____ jeans in class.
   (name)   (never)

5. _____ and _____ _____
   (name)   (name)   (usually)
   happy.

Exercise 8

Circle the correct words in the questions. Write answers. Use the
adverbs. Write complete sentences.

1. Where do you usually have (lunch   the lunch) during the week?

   _____

2. Why (you are   are you) sometimes unhappy?

   _____

3. Where do you often shop for (foods   food)?

   _____

4. Usually, how (is   are) the weather (in   at   on) winter in your city?

   _____

5. What do you never (eat   eats) for breakfast?

   _____

6. Where do you rarely go (in the   at) night?

   _____

Exercise 9

Start with names of people you know. Add the verb *be* when
necessary. Complete the sentences with your own ideas.

1. _____ always plays _____.
2. _____ and _____ never eat _____.
3. _____ often hungry _____.
4. _____ usually drives _____.
5. _____ sometimes does _____.

Possessive Adjectives and Possessive Nouns

Alma's hair is black, and her eyes are brown.

Singular Pronoun	Possessive Adjective	Plural Pronoun	Possessive Adjective
I	my	we	our
you	your	you	your
he	his		
she	her	they	their
it	its		

Possessive Adjective + Noun

Examples: My class is in Room 209.

Is your brother here?

Carmelo is a basketball player. His hands are very big.

That's our new neighbor. Her name is Alisa.

This is a fast car, but its engine is very efficient.

Our teacher is from Canada.

My neighbors work. Their children are in daycare.

Possessive Nouns = Noun + 's

Examples: Maria's car
Mike and Nancy's house
yesterday's newspaper

Possessive Form of Words Ending in *s:*

Examples: Carlos' job
(or)
Carlos's job

all the students' chairs

many countries' leaders

Possessive Question Word: *Whose?*

Example: Whose pen is this?
It's Makiko's pen. (or) It's Makiko's.

Exercise 1

Circle the correct words.

1. Mr. and Mrs. Sokolov have two cars. (They   His   Their) cars are old.

2. (Theresa   Theresas   Theresa's) husband likes (he   his) job.

3. There aren't any students from Europe in (Charles   Charles's) class.
   There are two European students in (we   our) class.

4. Russian is a difficult language. (It   Its) is hard to pronounce, and
   (it   its) grammar is not easy.

5. (I   My) have (yesterday   yesterday's) homework. It's in (I   my) backpack.
   Do (you   your) have (you   your) homework?

6. Does (you   your) teacher know all the (student's   students') names?

Discuss

a. Do you have a car? Is your car old or new?
b. How many students from Europe are there in your class?
c. Does your teacher know everyone's name?
d. Is your first language difficult to pronounce?

Exercise 2

Complete the questions. Write answers with possessive adjectives:
my/your/his/her/its/our/their.

1. What is your _____grandfather's_____ favorite food?
    _____(grandfather)_____
    ___His favorite food is spaghetti.___

2. What is your _____ favorite clothing store?
    _____(friend)_____
    _____

3. What is your _____ first language?
    _____(teacher)_____
    _____

4. What are your _____ names?
    _____(parent)_____
    _____

5. What is _____ favorite season—winter, spring, summer, or fall?
    _____(you)_____
    _____

6. What time does _____ class begin?
    _____(you)_____
    _____

7. What is your _____ favorite sport?
    ___(brother / friend)___
    _____

8. Where do your _____ children go to school?
    _____(neighbors)_____
    _____

Discuss

a. What is your favorite food? Why do you like it?
b. Do you have a favorite clothing store? If yes, where is it?
   What things do you buy there?
c. What is your favorite sport? Do you watch it? Do you play it?

Exercise 3: Dictation

Listen to your teacher. Write the questions. Then answer with complete sentences.

1. Question: _Whose pen is this?_

   Answer: _It's Nori's pen._

2. Question: _____

   Answer: _____

3. Question: _____

   Answer: _____

4. Question: _____

   Answer: _____

5. Question: _____

   Answer: _____

6. Question: _____

   Answer: _____

Exercise 4

Fix any mistakes.

1. Where is the women bathroom?

2. The story is on todays newspaper.

3. She always talks about other people's problems.

4. Brad and Kelly's mother cooks well, but they father is not good cook.

5. My father birthday is in September.

6. We like we new apartment.

Exercise 5

Complete the sentences. Write about people you know. Use possessive nouns in the first blank.

1. _____My mother's_____ office is on _____Elm Street_____.

2. _____ car is _____.

3. _____ eyes are _____.

4. _____ hometown is _____.

5. _____ grades in school are usually _____.

6. _____ job is very _____.

7. _____ favorite colors are _____.

Exercise 6

Complete the questions. Write answers. Use your classmates' names or the word *nobody.*

1. In your class, whose name _____ difficult?
   (be)

   _____

2. Whose eyes _____ blue?
   (be)

   _____

3. Whose favorite food _____ pizza?
   (be)

   _____

4. Whose country _____ a lot of oil?
   (have)

   _____

5. Whose pants _____ yellow?
   (be)

   _____

6. Whose children _____ English?
   (speak)

   _____

Exercise 7

Look at the pictures. Write possessive nouns and possessive adjectives with the noun shown in the picture.

1. <u>Juan's bicycle</u>
   (Juan)
   <u>his bicycle</u>

2. _____
   (Susanna)
   _____

3. _____
   (Mr. and Mrs. Lucas)
   _____

4. _____
   (my country)
   _____

5. _____
   (my teacher)
   _____

6. _____
   (the children)
   _____

Exercise 8

Write sentences. Use the words below the line. Add other words
when necessary. Use some possessives.

1. _____
   (Anita and Leo / often visit / daughter)

   _____
   (she / live / another city)

2. _____
   (we / like / neighbors)

   _____
   (they / be / very friendly)

3. _____
   (that store / be not / in use now)

   _____
   (windows / be / very dirty)

4. _____
   (brother / be / auto mechanic)

   _____
   (hands / often / get dirty)

Discuss

a. Do you like your neighbors? Are they friendly?
b. Where do your parents live? Is their home near or far?
c. Are there many stores near your school?
d. Do you know a good mechanic? Who?

Exercise 9

Write sentences with the words given.

1. our teacher's

   _____

2. my country's

   _____

3. their

   _____

4. our

   _____

Exercise 10

You will interview a partner. Complete the questions first. Then ask
your partner the questions. Write sentences about your partner. Use
possessive adjectives or possessive nouns.

1. Question: _____ *What is your* _____ name?

   Answer: My partner's name is _____.

2. Question: _____ home country?

   Answer: _____ home country is _____.

3. Question: _____ first language?

   Answer: _____ first language is _____.

4. Question: _____ birthday?

   Answer: _____ birthday is _____.

5. Question: _____ married or single?

   Answer: _____ is _____.

6. Question: _____ any brothers, sisters, or children?

   Answer: _____ has _____.

7. Question: _____ job?

   Answer: _____ job is _____.

8. Question: _____ favorite things to do?

   Answer: _____ likes _____.

20 *Yes/No* and *Or* Questions with Present-Tense Verbs

Do you have a car? Yes, I do.

Yes/No Questions and Short Answers with *Be*

Examples: Are you a student? Yes, I am.
Is the class easy? No, it isn't.
Are they at school now? Yes, they are.

Yes/No Questions with *Do/Does*

Do I . . . ?
Do you . . . ?
Does he/she/it . . . ?
Do we . . . ?
Do they . . . ?

Do/Does Questions and Short Answers

Examples: Do I have to come?   Yes, you do.   (or)   No, you don't.
Do you speak English?   Yes, I do.   (or)   No, I don't.
Does it snow much here?   Yes, it does.   (or)   No, it doesn't.
Does Nina like the snow?   Yes, she does.   (or)   No, she doesn't.
Do you all usually do your homework? Yes, we do.   (or)   No, we don't.
Do they live in New York?   Yes, they do.   (or)   No, they don't.

Or Questions and Answers with *Be*

Examples: Is the party on Friday or Saturday? It's on Friday.
Are you ready or not? I'm ready.
Is your car here or at home? It's here.

Or Questions with Other Verbs

Examples: Do you usually cook or do you go out? I usually cook.
Does she work in the morning or in the evening? In the morning.
Do they have an apartment or a house? They have a house.

Exercise 1: Dictation

Listen to your teacher. Write the questions. Then write short answers. Discuss with a partner.

1. Question: _____

   Answer: _____

2. Question: _____

   Answer: _____

3. Question: _____

   Answer: _____

4. Question: _____

   Answer: _____

Exercise 2

Circle the correct words. Then write short answers. Discuss with
a partner.

1. Question: (You   Do you   Are you) like (spicy food   food spicy)?

   Answer: _____

2. Question: (Are you   Do you) left-handed (and   or) right-handed?

   Answer: _____

3. Question: (Is   Do   Are   Does) your classmates (speak   speaks) English?

   Answer: _____

4. Question: (You   Are you   Do you) (shop usually   usually shop)

   (in   on) the weekend?

   Answer: _____

Exercise 3

Fix any mistakes in the questions. Write short answers. Discuss with
a partner.

1. Question: Do you usually tired in morning?

   Answer: _____

2. Question: Does your teacher wears jeans in class?

   Answer: _____

3. Question: Are your friends live in a apartment or a house?

   Answer: _____

4. Question: Is the air in your city clean?

   Answer: _____

5. Question: Is your teacher have black hair?

   Answer: _____

Exercise 4

**Complete the questions. Add and change words when necessary.
Then write short answers. Discuss with a partner.**

1. _____ how to cook?
   (your father / know)
   _____

2. _____ glasses?
   (anyone / family / wear)
   _____

3. _____ a lot of coffee?
   (people / family / drink)
   _____

4. _____ cheap or expensive?
   (gasoline / be)
   _____

5. _____ any pets?
   (you / have)
   _____

6. _____ the bus to work?
   (you / drive / ride)
   _____

Exercise 5

Write questions. Use the words given. Add and change words when
necessary. Write short answers. Discuss with a partner.

1. you / like / action movies

   Question: _____

   Answer: _____

2. there / lot / people from other countries / your city

   Question: _____

   Answer: _____

3. your teacher / usually / give / homework / weekend

   Question: _____

   Answer: _____

4. your first name / common

   Question: _____

   Answer: _____

Exercise 6

Read the answer. Then write the question.

1. Question: _Do you speak Chinese?_____
   Answer: No, I don't speak Chinese.

2. Question: _____
   Answer: Yes, I like Italian food.

3. Question: _____
   Answer: Yes, my hometown has an airport.

4. Question: _____
   Answer: No, my classmates don't smoke.

5. Question: _____ or _____?
   Answer: The movie begins at 7 p.m., not at 6 p.m.

Exercise 7

Complete the questions. Use the names of classmates or famous people. Write short answers. Discuss with a partner.

1. Question: _____ sometimes sleep in class?

   Answer: _____

2. Question: _____ play tennis?

   Answer: _____

3. Question: _____ have a good voice?

   Answer: _____

4. Question: _____ and _____ often study together?

   Answer: _____

5. Question: _____ quiet or talkative?

   Answer: _____

6. Question: _____ and _____ work together?

   Answer: _____

 *Wh-* Questions with Present-Tense Verbs

How many children do they have?

Some *Wh-* Question Words and Phrases

who
whom
what
where
when
why
which
how
what color
what time
what kind of
how much
how many
how long
how old

Wh- Questions with the Verb *Be*

Question word + *am/is/are* + subject
Examples: Where are you?

How long is the movie?

Who is she?

Wh- Questions with Other Verbs

Question word + *do/does* + subject + verb
Examples: Where do you work?

What time does class begin?

How do you spell your name?

Where do you (all) live?

Why does he get up so early?

Who does Maria play chess with?

How often do your cousins visit you?

Wh- Question Word as Subject

Examples: Who lives here?

How many live here?

What happened?

Exercise 1: Dictation

**Listen to your teacher. Write the questions. Then write answers.
Discuss with a partner.**

1. Question: _____

   Answer: _____

2. Question: _____

   Answer: _____

3. Question: _____

   Answer: _____

4. Question: _____

   Answer: _____

Exercise 2

Circle the correct words. Write answers. Discuss with a partner.

1. Question: Where (do   does   is   are) your classmates (do   make) (they   their   his) homework?

   Answer: _____

2. Question: (How much   How many) (is   does) a new computer (costs   cost)?

   Answer: _____

3. Question: (What   How) (you are   are you   do you) afraid of?

   Answer: _____

4. Question: Which restaurant (is   are   do   does) (you   your) favorite?

   Answer: _____

5. Question: (What   How often) (are   do) you clean your home?

   Answer: _____

Exercise 3

Fix any mistakes in the questions. Then write answers.

1. Question: When are you go to bed in the weekend?

   Answer: _____

2. Question: Why you is in this class?

   Answer: _____

3. Question: Where does the teacher lives?

   Answer: _____

4. Question: In your class, who does usually sit next to the door?

   Answer: _____

5. Question: How many teeth do most people have?

   Answer: _____

Exercise 4

**Complete the questions. Use the verb *be* or other verbs.
Then write answers.**

1. Question: What color _____ your favorite shoes?

   Answer: _____

2. Question: Where _____ you usually _____

   after class?

   Answer: _____

3. Question: In your class, who _____ fast?

   Answer: _____

4. Question: What kind of car _____ your neighbor

   _____?

   Answer: _____

Exercise 5

**Write questions. Use the words given. Answer with
complete sentences.**

1. like / for / What / you / dessert? / do

   Question: _____

   Answer: _____

2. home / far / from school? / How / your / is

   Question: _____

   Answer: _____

3. do / today? / How / you / feel

   Question: _____

   Answer: _____

Exercise 6

Look at the pictures. Complete the questions and write answers.

1. Where ___does she_____ study?

   _____

2. What _____ the library close?

   _____

3. Why _____ happy?

   _____

4. How _____ children does he have?

   _____

5. How _____ it cost?

   _____

6. Why _____ so cheap?

   _____

7. What game_____ play?

   _____

8. When _____ leave?

   _____

Exercise 7

**Complete the questions. Use names of people you know.
Then write answers.**

1. Question: Where __does Andre_____ work?

   Answer: ___He works downtown in a government office._____

2. Question: What _____ dream about?

   Answer: _____

3. Question: When _____ and _____ exercise?

   Answer: _____

4. Question: What kind of clothes _____ wear to work?

   Answer: _____

Exercise 8

**Write questions. Use the words given. Add and change words when
necessary. Then write answers.**

1. anyone in your family / play / musical instrument?

   Question: _____

   Answer: _____

2. what time / your / get home from work?

   Question: _____

   Answer: _____

3. what / your teacher / favorite word?

   Question: _____

   Answer: _____

4. how many / book / you / have / your house?

   Question: _____

   Answer: _____

Exercise 9

Write questions. Use the words given, and complete the questions with your own ideas. Then write answers.

1. What kind of movies do . . . ?

   Question: _____

   Answer: _____

2. What time does . . . ?

   Question: _____

   Answer: _____

3. Where do . . . ?

   Question: _____

   Answer: _____

Exercise 10

Write a *wh-* question for each topic. Write answers. Then discuss with a partner.

1. music

   Question: _____

   Answer: _____

2. school

   Question: _____

   Answer: _____

3. the Internet

   Question: _____

   Answer: _____

4. free time

   Question: _____

   Answer: _____

Present-Tense Negative Verbs

22

He does not have any money.

Affirmative and Negative Verbs

Examples: I speak English. I do not speak Swedish.
      This bus does not go downtown. It goes to the mall.

Negative Form of Present-Tense Verbs: *do/does + not + verb*

I do not + verb
you do not + verb
he/she/it does not + verb
we do not + verb
they do not + verb
Examples: I do not live in a big house.
      You do not need a new car.
      She does not work at night.
      We do not want more homework.
      They do not use their computer very much.

Contractions

do not = don't
does not = doesn't
Examples: I don't know.
You don't live here.
He doesn't smoke.
We don't like cheese.
They don't watch TV often.

Negative Form of the Verb *Be: be + not*

Examples: I am not usually hungry in the morning.
You are not late today.
She is not my sister.
We are not in class this week.
It is not cold.
They are not at home.

Exercise 1: Dictation

Listen to the teacher. Write the sentences.

1. _____

2. _____

3. _____

4. _____

5. _____

Discuss

a. Do you go to school on the weekend?
b. Do you know which is the official language in Brazil? In what countries is Spanish the official language?
c. Does your home country have a king? What countries have a king?
d. Do police in your home country carry guns? Do you have a gun?
e. Are government offices in your city open on the weekend? What other places are closed on the weekend?

Exercise 2

Circle the correct words.

1. Vegetarians (not eat   do not eat   no eat) meat. (He   They) (eat   eats) fruit, bread, nuts, and vegetables.

2. A candy bar (don't cost   isn't cost   doesn't cost) much money. (It   He   She) (cost   costs) about $1.00.

3. Switzerland (no have   isn't have   doesn't have) a big army. (His   Its   An) army is (a small   small).

4. Many people (in   at   on) Vietnam (aren't   don't) drive cars. (He   They   It) (are ride   ride   rides) bikes or motorcycles.

> ### Discuss
> a. Do you know any vegetarians?
> b. Do you eat candy bars very often?
> c. Does your home country have a big army?
> d. Do people in your home country ride motorcycles? Do they ride bikes?

Exercise 3

Fix any mistakes.

1. I don't from English-speaking country. My first language not English.

2. Many smalls streets in Japan doesn't have names.

3. Baseball does not popular in Africa, but it popular in United States.

4. Mohammed is a Muslim. He doesn't eat pork.

5. Some people no like loud music. He like quiet music.

> ### Discuss
> a. What is your first language? Do you think English is easy?
> b. What street do you live on? Is it a big or a small street?
> c. Do you like baseball? Is it popular in your home country?
> d. Is there any food you don't eat?
> e. Do you like loud music?

Exercise 4

Fill in the blanks to make true statements. Use the verbs in the list.
Use affirmative and negative forms.

> ✔be   be   be   have   listen   speak   work

1. Sushi _____ *is not* _____ a typical American food.

   It _____ *is* _____ a Japanese food.

2. Most people in Algeria _____ English.

   They _____ Arabic or French.

3. Canberra _____ the capital of Austria.

   It _____ the capital of Australia.

4. A bicycle _____ four wheels.

   It _____ two wheels.

5. Whales _____ mammals.

   They _____ fish.

6. We _____ on the weekend.

   We _____ from Monday to Friday.

7. I _____ to music in class.

   I _____ to music outside of class.

Discuss

a. Where is Algeria? Are you sure?
b. Do you know people who speak Arabic? Where are they from?
c. Do you know which city is the capital of Austria?
d. Do you have a bicycle?
e. How many days a week do you work?
f. Do you ever listen to music in class?

Exercise 5

Complete the questions. Then write two sentences to answer each question. First write a short answer. Then write another sentence.

1. you / have / a new car?

   Question: _Do you have a new car?_

   Answer: _No, I don't. My car is three years old._
   (or)
   Answer: _Yes, I do. I have a new car._

2. you / work / in a restaurant?

   Question: _____

   Answer: _____

3. it / rain / in your city every day?

   Question: _____

   Answer: _____

4. your parents / be / in Europe now?

   Question: _____

   Answer: _____

5. your neighborhood / have / a swimming pool?

   Question: _____

   Answer: _____

6. your relatives / call / you very often?

   Question: _____

   Answer: _____

7. you be / allergic to anything?

   Question: _____

   Answer: _____

Exercise 6

Write two sentences. In the first sentence, use the words given. Then write a related sentence.

1. we / not have

   We do not have class on Sunday.

   We have class from Monday to Friday.

2. my son / not have

   _____

   _____

3. I / not go

   _____

   _____

4. our teacher / be not

   _____

   _____

5. many children / not like

   _____

   _____

6. cats / be not

   _____

   _____

7. I / not remember

   _____

   _____

8. we / not know

   _____

   _____

Present Progressive Tense

Shhh! They're sleeping!

Present Progressive = now/at this time

Examples: It rains a lot in Seattle, but right now the sun is shining.
Adeyemi loves seafood. He's cooking shrimp right now.
My aunt and uncle travel a lot. Right now, they are visiting Ireland.

Form of Present Progressive: *be (am/is/are)* + verb + *-ing*

Examples: I am now living in an apartment on Third Street.
He is studying at the library.
They are building a new house.

Questions: *Wh-* question word + *be (am/is/are)* + subject + verb + *-ing*

Examples: Is she still working at the Accounting Office?
How are you feeling today?
Where are they going?

Negative: *be (am/is/are) + not + verb + -ing*

Examples: I'm not using my computer right now.
You are not doing it right.
She isn't playing very well right now.

Exceptions

Some verbs don't usually use present progressive. Here are some of these verbs:
believe
have
see, hear
forget, remember
know, understand
like, love
need, want
Examples: I need some help. (right now)
What do you see? (now)

Spelling

cut—cutting
meet—meeting
make—making
play—playing
lie—lying
happen—happening
occur—occurring

Exercise 1: Dictation

Listen to your teacher. Write the sentences.

1. _____ present progressive _____.

2. _____

3. _____

4. _____

5. _____

6. _____

7. _____

Exercise 2

Write the *-ing* form of each verb.

1. look: _looking_

2. sit: _____

3. make: _____

4. watch: _____

5. begin: _____

6. write: _____

7. carry: _____

8. eat: _____

9. forget: _____

Exercise 3

Circle the correct words.

1. We (planning   are plan   are planning) a trip (at   to   on) Las Vegas
   (in   at   on) April.

2. I (am not   don't want   not wanting) (a   an) old car.

3. Why (you are   are you) (wear   wearing) (sunglass   sunglasses)?

4. The children (is not   are not   do not) (sleep   sleeping   sleeps) now.
   (He   They) (watch   are watching   do watch) TV.

5. (Do you   Are you) (see   seeing) the smoke over there? Maybe
   (is   there is   there are) a fire.

6. Turn (on   in) the heater, please. (It   He) (is getting   gets   getting)
   cold in here.

Discuss

a. Are you planning a trip?
b. Do you have a car? Are you shopping for a new one?
c. Is anyone in class wearing sunglasses now?
d. Is it getting cold in here?
e. What is the teacher doing now?

Exercise 4

Fix any mistakes.

1. What you are reading?

2. Right now, my daughter and his friend is shopping at the mall.

3. She not using the computer now. She talking in the phone.

4. I'm tired. I'm go to the bed now. Good night.

5. The sink in my apartment no is working, but the manager is fix it now.

Discuss

a. Do you like to read? If yes, are you reading anything for fun?
b. Do you shop at the mall?
c. What time do you go to bed on weekdays?
d. Can you fix broken things in your home? Is anything not working?

Exercise 5

Complete the sentences. Use the present progressive.

1. Nadia _____ to another city because she _____
   (move)   (not like)
   the weather here.

2. My neighbors _____ their house now. It _____
   (paint)   (look)
   good.

3. Right now, the teacher _____ a video to the class.
   (show)

4. She _____ well right now. Maybe she _____
   (not feel)   (have)
   a cold.

5. My kids _____ fast this year. They _____ tall.
   (grow)   (get)

6. Slow down! You _____ too fast!
   (drive)

Exercise 6

Look at the pictures. Write questions and answers. Use the present progressive.

1. Question: _What is she doing?_

   Answer: _She is driving the car._

2. Question: _____

   Answer: _____

3. Question: _____

   Answer: _____

4. Question: _____

   Answer: _____

5. Question: _____

   Answer: _____

6. Question: _____

   Answer: _____

7. Question: _____

   Answer: _____

8. Question: _____

   Answer: _____

Exercise 7

Write questions. Write the answers. Then discuss with a partner.

1. What / teacher / do / right now?

   Question: _What is the teacher doing right now?_

   Answer: _She is talking to Oskar._

2. Why / you / study English?

   Question: _____

   Answer: _____

3. How many people / live / your home / now?

   Question: _____

   Answer: _____

4. the sun / shine / right now?

   Question: _____

   Answer: _____

5. What time / you / usually / get up / morning?

   Question: _____

   Answer: _____

6. Who / sit / next to / you right now?

   Question: _____

   Answer: _____

7. you / usually / speak English with your friends?

   Question: _____

   Answer: _____

8. What / you / think about / right now?

   Question: _____

   Answer: _____

Exercise 8

Complete the sentences.

1. Right now, the council _____ the traffic problem.
   (discuss)

2. Every year, the council _____ the traffic problem.
   (discuss)

3. She always _____ to the supermarket on Saturday morning.
   (go)

4. She _____ to the doctor right now.
   (go)

5. I _____ a job now.
   (look for)

6. _____ a job every summer?
   (you / look for)

7. Usually, it _____ here in the spring.
   (not snow)

8. _____ now?
   (it / snow)

Exercise 9

**Look around. Write sentences that tell what you see and hear.
What is happening? What are people doing?**

1. _Frida is talking to Ali._ _____

2. _____

3. _____

4. _____

5. _____

6. _____

7. _____

8. _____

Connectors
And, But, Or, So

Bernardo doesn't have a car, so he takes a bus to school.

Connecting Adjectives, Nouns, and Verbs

Examples: My car is big but slow.
We go to the beach or to the mountains every summer.
In the morning, she drinks coffee and reads the newspaper.

Connecting Sentences

Examples: Trees are beautiful, and they also produce oxygen.
She's rich, but she doesn't live in a big house.
He is sick, so he is staying in bed.
On Saturday morning, I go shopping, or I do my laundry.

Punctuation

Note comma use in the examples above.

Adjective/Noun/Verb *and/or/but* Adjective/Noun/Verb

Examples: Grammar is necessary but sometimes difficult.
Felipe and Rafael look like their mother.
In the evening, he watches TV or listens to music.

Subject + Verb, *and/but/or/so* Subject + Verb

Examples: Sophia's grandparents are from Italy, but she does not speak Italian.
They go to bed very late, so they are often tired.
On Sundays, I call my children, or they call me.

Exercise 1: Dictation

Write the sentences your teacher reads. Use correct punctuation.

1. Hong Kong is part of China, so people from Hong Kong
    speak Chinese.

2. _____

    _____

3. _____

    _____

4. _____

    _____

5. _____

    _____

Discuss

a. What other language do many people in Hong Kong speak?
b. Who in your family does not speak English?
c. Do you have children or brothers or sisters? Do they speak English?
d. What other languages do students in your home country study?
e. Do you usually have homework? How long do you study every evening?

Exercise 2

Circle the correct words. Check punctuation.

1. Some people (eat   eats   are eat) a lot of (meat but   meat, but) too much meat (is not   does not   no is) good for your health.

2. Mr. Garcia (is   has) 79 years (old   , old   old,) and he (no is   is not   do not) very healthy.

3. My (roommate   roommates   roommate's) eyes (isn't   aren't) very good, (but   so) she (is wear   wear   wears) glasses.

4. She (drinks never   never drinks) milk, (so   or   but) (she   her   your) bones (no are   do not   are not) strong.

5. For dessert, eat some fruit, like (a   an) apple (or   , or) a banana, not cake.

> ### Discuss
> a. Is everyone in your family healthy?
> b. Do you have good eyes and ears?
> c. Do you drink much milk?
> d. Do you have a favorite kind of meat?
> e. What do you like for dessert?

Exercise 3

Fix any mistakes. Check for grammar and punctuation.

1. Small cars not have big engines so it do not use much gasoline.

2. Big cars fast but, they use a lot a gasoline.

3. Small cars are cheap to drive, and they do not pollute like big cars.

4. Both my father and mother have a small cars.

5. Small cars are not expensive. So many people like them.

> ### Discuss
> a. Do you have a car?
> b. If yes, is your car big, small, or mid-sized?
> c. What kinds of cars do you like? Why do you like them?

Exercise 4

Complete the sentences. Add and change words when necessary.

1. Computers are important in many jobs, and _____ easy to use.

(be)

2. A new computer can be expensive, but _____ cheap computers too.

(there / be)

3. Some people don't like computers, so _____ them in their homes.

(not have)

4. Computers are difficult for some adults, but _____

(you / never too old)

to learn something new.

Exercise 5

Complete the sentences. Then combine them.

1. _____*Fuyuko*_____ is very nice.

(name)

_____*She*_____ _____*is*_____ also intelligent.

(pronoun) (be)

*Fuyuko is very nice, and she is also intelligent.*

2. _____ is a good student.

(name)

_____ sometimes _____ to class late.

(pronoun) (come)

_____

3. _____ studies a lot.

(name)

_____ always _____ good grades.

(pronoun) (get)

_____

4. _____ and _____ are friends.

(name) (name)

They _____ the same language.

(not speak)

_____

5. _____ doesn't cook well.

(name)

_____ often _____ in restaurants.

(pronoun) (eat)

_____

Exercise 6

Write sentences. Remember to punctuate correctly.

1. the Sahara Desert / be / big desert / Africa

   _____

2. not rain / much in the Sahara Desert / so / very dry

   _____

3. there / not many animal / tree / plant / the Sahara Desert

   _____

4. some people / live / there / but / their life / be not easy

   _____

Exercise 7

Complete the questions and write answers. Use a connector in each answer. Then discuss with a partner.

1. When _<u>do you usually go</u>_____ to bed?

   (you usually / go)

   _<u>I usually go to bed at 11:00, but sometimes I go to bed at 12:00 or 1:00.</u>___

2. Where _____ dinner?

   (you usually / eat)

   _____

3. _____ large, small, or medium-sized?

   (your home)

   _____

4. What time _____?

   (class / usually end)

   _____

5. What _____ in the evening?

   (you usually / do)

   _____

6. _____ to exercise?

   (you / like)

   _____

Exercise 8

Write complete sentences. Use correct punctuation.

1. My first language / so

   _____

   _____

2. My favorite food / but

   _____

   _____

3. My friends like / and they

   _____

   _____

4. On the weekend, I usually / or my friends and I

   _____

   _____

5. This city is / so

   _____

   _____

6. My family is / and

   _____

   _____

7. My / but my

   _____

   _____

Past Tense

He didn't go to the party last night because he was sick.

Past Tense of Regular Verbs: verb + *-ed*

Examples: talk—talked
show—showed

Negative Past Tense: *did not/didn't* + verb

Examples: did not talk   (or)   didn't talk
did not have   (or)   didn't have

Questions: *did* + subject + verb

Examples: Did you eat?
Where did you go?

Short Answers

Examples: Yes, I did.
No, you didn't.
Yes, he did.
No, they didn't.

Past Tense of Some Irregular Verbs

Present	Past
buy	bought
come	came
cost	cost
do	did
eat	ate
get	got
give	gave
go	went
have	had
leave	left
put	put
read	read
say	said
see	saw
take	took
write	wrote

Past Tense of the Verb *Be*

Present	Past	Negative	Question
I am	I was	I was not	Was I . . . ?
you are	you were	you were not	Were you . . . ?
he/she/it is	he/she/it was	he/she/it was not	Was he . . . ?
we are	we were	we were not	Were we . . . ?
you are	you were	you were not	Were you . . . ?
they are	they were	they were not	Were they . . . ?

Some Past Time Expressions

in 1965
last week
3 months ago

Exercise 1: Dictation

Listen to your teacher. Write the sentences.

1. _____
2. _____
3. _____
4. _____

Exercise 2

Circle the correct answers.

1. Yesterday, the teacher (says   said), "Your tests (was   were) very good."

2. (The last   Last) night, I (was not eat   did not eat   did not ate) dinner because I (am not   was not   did not) hungry.

3. (Do you   Did you   were you) (go   went) shopping last weekend?

4. Why (he was   was he) so quiet yesterday? Because he (has   had   was) (headache   a headache).

> ### Discuss
> a. What did you eat for dinner last night?
> b. Did you go shopping last weekend? What did you buy?
> c. Did you have a headache yesterday? Do you often have headaches?

Exercise 3

Fix any mistakes.

1. My parents give me new car for my last birthday.

2. She look for a apartment last weekend, but she didn't found anything.

3. In 1776, there were only 13 American states, but now there are 50.

4. Where you put the cars keys yesterday? I leaved them on the table.

5. Oh, sorry! I was write the wrong date in my check.

Exercise 4

Complete the sentences. Use the verbs in the box.

be	be	eat	not have	play
be	drive	listen	not read	walk

1. Last night, I _____ dinner early because I _____ hungry.

2. When we _____ young, we _____ to school, but now we _____ our cars.

3. He _____ the paper because he _____ time.

4. They _____ soccer last Saturday, so on Sunday they _____ tired.

5. _____ you _____ to the radio last night?

Discuss

a. What time do you usually have dinner? What time did you eat yesterday?
b. How did you go to school when you were young?
c. Do you usually read the paper? Did you read today's paper?
d. What sport did you play when you were young?

Exercise 5

Fill in the blanks.

1. My parents _____ married when they _____ young.
   (get)   (be)

2. I _____ the homework last night.
   (not do)

3. Last week, two students _____ to class late, and one student
   (come)
   _____ absent.
   (be)

4. Every morning, my friend _____ bread.
   (make)

5. When I _____ young, my family _____ a dog.
   (be)   (not have)

Exercise 6

Write sentences or questions. Add and change words when necessary.

1. last Monday / they / wait / long time / the doctor's office.

   _____

2. where / you / get / your watch?

   _____

3. who / write / *Romeo and Juliet?*

   _____

4. United States / buy / Alaska / from Russia / many years ago.

   _____

5. she always / take / shower / before / she / go / work.

   _____

6. last weekend / I / go / the beach / with my friends.

   _____

7. I / not / go / my friend / party / last night

   _____

8. no one / my family / speak English / when I / be / child.

   _____

Discuss

a. When was your last visit to the doctor?
b. Did you read *Romeo and Juliet?* If yes, when?
c. Did you know that Russia once owned Alaska?
d. What did you do last weekend?
e. When did you last go to the beach?
f. When you were young, did anyone speak English in your home?

Exercise 7

Look at the pictures. Complete the questions. Then write complete answers.

1. When _____ to bed last night?

(you / go)

   _____

2. How much _____?

(your book / cost)

   _____

3. What _____ for your last birthday?

(you / get)

   _____

4. Where _____ yesterday at 7 p.m.?

(you / be)

   _____

5. _____ a movie last week?

(you / see)

   _____

6. Where _____?

(you / grow up)

   _____

26 Can and Will

I can't finish now. I will do this tomorrow.

Meaning

can = ability/permission
will = future

Form: *can/will* + verb

Examples: She can speak English.
I will call you tomorrow.

Contractions with *will*

I will = I'll
you will = you'll
he will = he'll
we will = we'll
they will = they'll
Example: I will call you. = I'll call you.

Negatives and Negative Contractions

cannot = can't

will not = won't

Examples: You cannot do that.   (or)   You can't do that.

          They will not buy the books.   (or)   They won't buy the books.

Question: *Can/will* + subject + verb

Examples: Can she speak Japanese?

          Will you have time next week?

Short Answers

Examples: Yes, she can.   (or)   No, she cannot.   (or)   No, she can't.

          Yes, we will.   (or)   No, we will not.   (or)   No, we won't.

Will + Verb *be* + Adjective

Example: I will be busy next week.

Some Future Time Words

tomorrow

next month

this weekend

in three weeks

Exercise 1: Dictation

Listen to your teacher. Write the sentences.

1. _____

2. _____

3. _____

4. _____

Discuss

   a. Can you play soccer?

   b. Where will you be next year?

   c. Do you have a picture of your family?

   d. When are your classes finished today?

Exercise 2

Circle the correct words.

1. Many (people   peoples) in the world (can   are can) (speak   to speak) two (language   languages).

2. My brother (no can   cannot) (drive   to drive   drives) a car because (is   he is) too young.

3. When (you will   will you have   to have   be have) some free time?

4. (Maria   Marias   Maria's) plane (arrive   was arrive   arrived) late (last night   the last night), so today she (will tired   will be tired).

5. Why (you can't   can't you) (go   to go) (at   in   to) the party with me?

> ### Discuss
> a. How many languages can you speak?
> b. Can anyone in your family speak two or three languages?
> c. At what age can a person get a driver's license in the U.S.?
> d. When did you last fly on an airplane?

Exercise 3

Fix any mistakes.

1. When you will be back?

2. They can't to get married until the next year.

3. In 50 years, the world will very different.

4. Why can't he get a job?

5. Can you to help me, please?

6. On this weekend, we won't has many free time.

> ### Discuss
> a. What will be one change in the world in the future?
> b. How will your life be different next year?
> c. Will this class help you get a job, or help you in your job?
> d. Will you be busy this weekend?

Exercise 4

Complete the questions. Then write answers.

1. _____ very well?
   (you / can cook)

   _____

2. How old _____ in the year 2025?
   (you / be)

   _____

3. Where _____ 5 years from now?
   (you / be)

   _____

4. In the future, _____ in this city?
   (you / stay)

   _____

5. What _____ well?
   (your classmates / can do)

   _____

Exercise 5

Complete the sentences.

1. He _____ ,
   (can / not / swim)

   so next summer he _____ swimming lessons.
   (take)

2. Maybe in the year 2050, there _____ flying cars.
   (be)

3. My friend _____ usually late, so tomorrow he probably
   (be)

   _____ on time.
   (not be)

4. Why _____ me last night?
   (you / not / call)

5. _____ me tomorrow?
   (you / call)

Discuss

a. Can you swim? If yes, how well can you swim?
b. Are you usually on time or late?
c. Did anyone call you last night?

Exercise 6

Write sentences. Add and change words when necessary.

1. don't / late / tomorrow / or the teacher / not / happy

   _____

2. where / you / be / this time next year?

   _____

3. why / we / can't buy / new car?

   _____

4. we / not have / enough money / for a new car

   _____

5. it / not snow / last night / so we can / not ski / today

   _____

Exercise 7

Complete the sentences. Write about people you know.

1. _____ can _____ very well.

2. _____ and _____ cannot _____

   because _____ .

3. Tomorrow, _____ won't _____ because

   _____ .

4. In the year 2020, _____ will probably be _____

   because _____ .

5. Can _____ ?

6. Will _____ ?

Exercise 8

Write complete sentences. Use the words given and your own ideas.

1. My friend cannot / because

   _____

   _____

2. The teacher can / because

   _____

   _____

3. I won't / because

   _____

   _____

4. Many people in my home country can't / because

   _____

   _____

5. Next weekend, I won't / because

   _____

   _____

6. One hundred years from now

   _____

   _____

7. My classmates can / and they

   _____

   _____

8. Next year, we

   _____

   _____

Dictations

Replace words in brackets with appropriate information for your students.

Introductory Unit B: Four Important Questions (Exercise 2)

1. right
2. boxes
3. giraffe
4. yellow
5. jump

Introductory Unit C: Basic Punctuation (Exercise 1)

1. Today is [month/date/year].
2. It is [hot/cool/sunny/cloudy/rainy/etc.] today.
3. What time is it?
4. It's [time].
5. My teacher's name is [Mr./Mrs./Ms.] [family name].
6. [His/Her] first language is [language].
7. A gallon of gasoline is [approximate current price].

Introductory Unit D: Questions and Question Words (Exercise 2)

1. How are you today?
2. What is your name?
3. Are you a student?
4. Who is your teacher?
5. What time is your class?
6. Are you single or married?
7. Where are you from?
8. Why are you in this class?
9. When is your birthday?
10. Do you have a computer?

Unit 1: *I, My, You, Your* (Exercise 1)

1. I'm hungry.
2. My first language is not English.
3. Where is your car?
4. You are a good student.

Unit 2: Subject Pronouns (Exercise 1)

1. I'm ready for class. Are you ready?
2. The book is long, but it is good.
3. My cousin and I are together often. We are good friends.
4. Mrs. Selig is Canadian. She is from Toronto.
5. Mr. Tran is not here today. Is he ill?
6. Computers are necessary, but they are expensive.

Unit 3: Singular and Plural Nouns (Exercise 1)

1. table
2. house
3. party
4. friend
5. day
6. woman
7. match

Unit 4: Adjectives (Exercise 1)

1. new shoes
2. green tea
3. my good friend
4. expensive cars
5. a difficult language

Unit 5: Demonstratives (Exercise 2)

[Note to teacher: Point to things in the classroom as you read the sentences.]
1. This is my pencil.
2. Those books are in English.
3. These are coins.
4. That window is [open/closed].
5. This [chair/desk] is [old/new].

Unit 6: The Verb *Be* (Exercise 1)

1. This book is in English.
2. U.S. dollars are green.
3. I'm sorry I'm late.
4. OK, we're ready.
5. You're my best friend.
6. Some people are worried.

Unit 7: Negative of the Verb *Be* (Exercise 1)

1. My teacher is not from [country].
2. Textbooks are not cheap.
3. We aren't busy today.
4. It isn't [day of the week].
5. I'm not sure.

Unit 8: Prepositions of Time (Exercise 1)

1. in the evening
2. in June
3. at 6:40 p.m.
4. in the morning
5. on May 13
6. at night
7. on Thursday
8. in 1987

Unit 9: *Yes/No* and *Or* Questions with the Verb *Be* (Exercise 1)

1. Are you an American citizen?
2. Is your home country big or small?
3. Is your first name a common name?
4. Are people in your city friendly or unfriendly?
5. Are airports busy on weekends?
6. Is gasoline expensive?

Unit 10: *Wh-* Questions with the Verb *Be* (Exercise 1)

1. What is the capital of China?
2. Where is your book?
3. How many students are there in your class?
4. When is Valentine's Day?
5. Which month is your favorite?

Unit 11: Count and Noncount Nouns (Exercise 1)

1. It's an old house.
2. Some German cars are expensive.
3. A soccer ball is black and white.
4. Do you have any money from your country?

Unit 12: *There Is* and *There Are* (Exercise 1)

1. There are a lot of trains in Europe.
2. There's a lot of traffic in Tokyo.
3. There are no [Americans/Brazilians/etc.] in our class.
4. Is there a desert in your country?
5. There aren't any classes on Sunday.
6. Are there any supermarkets near your home?

Unit 13: Imperatives (Exercise 1)

1. Please sit down.
2. Don't forget your keys.
3. Please speak English with me.
4. Do this page for homework.
5. Don't be late for class!
6. Put out the trash, please.
7. Turn on the lights.

Unit 14: Present Tense of Verbs (Exercise 1)

1. Babies drink milk.
2. Mrs. Lee takes a bus to work.
3. We do homework every day.
4. I live in [city or town].
5. It snows a lot in Canada in winter.

Unit 15: Present Tense: Third Person Singular -*s* (Exercise 1)

1. The U.S. president lives in Washington, D.C.
2. It rains a lot in Tokyo in spring.
3. A new car costs a lot of money.
4. The word *huge* means "very big."
5. He takes the bus to school.

Unit 16: Present Tense: *Be* and Other Verbs (Exercise 1)

1. Many people in Holland speak English.
2. It is not very cold in Taiwan in the winter.
3. Cairo and Shanghai are big cities.
4. My friends live in the mountains.

Unit 17: Prepositions of Place (Exercise 1)

1. They're in class now.
2. He's on vacation now in Spain.
3. Is he at home now?
4. The mall [is far/isn't very far] from here.

Unit 18: Adverbs of Frequency (Exercise 6)

1. It is never hot in the Sahara Desert in the summer.
2. Babies seldom cry.
3. The sun sometimes rises in the west.
4. Brazil rarely has a good soccer team.
5. Our teacher seldom gives homework.

Unit 19: Possessive Adjectives and Possessive Nouns (Exercise 3)

1. Whose pen is this?
2. What color is [student's name] hair ?
3. [Hold up a student's book.] Whose book is this?
4. Are [student's name] and [student's name] shoes the same size ?
5. [Hold up someone's glasses.] Whose glasses are these?
6. Are your parents' eyes blue?

Unit 20: *Yes/No* and *Or* Questions with Present-Tense Verbs (Exercise 1)

1. Do you live alone?
2. Does it rain much here?
3. Do you have any relatives in this city?
4. On Friday night, do you usually go out, or do you stay home?

Unit 21: *Wh-* Questions with Present-Tense Verbs (Exercise 1)

1. When do you get up on weekdays?
2. What kind of music do you and your friends like?
3. Who in your class has a car?
4. Where is your friend from?

Unit 22: Present-Tense Negative Verbs (Exercise 1)

1. Many students don't go to school on the weekend.
2. Spanish is not the official language in Brazil.
3. Canada doesn't have a king.
4. Police in England do not carry guns.
5. Government offices aren't open on Sundays.

Unit 23: Present Progressive Tense (Exercise 1)

1. We're studying present progressive verbs.
2. It [is/isn't] raining right now.
3. What are you doing?
4. I don't believe you.
5. He's listening to some music.
6. Are they living together now?
7. This soup needs some salt.

Unit 24: Connectors (Exercise 1)

1. Hong Kong is part of China, so people from Hong Kong speak Chinese.
2. Many people work hard, but they don't make a lot of money.
3. Children are intelligent, and they learn languages fast.
4. A lot of students in the U.S. study Spanish or French.
5. We want to learn, so we study hard and do our homework.

Unit 25: Past Tense (Exercise 1)

1. I talked to my friend last weekend.
2. Yesterday, it was not very [hot/cold].
3. When I was young, I did not speak English.
4. Did we have homework last night?

Unit 26: *Can* and *Will* (Exercise 1)

1. They can both play soccer very well.
2. Will you be in this school next year?
3. She can't come to work because her son is sick.
4. I'll bring a picture of my family tomorrow.

Grammar Handbook

Introductory Unit B: Four Important Questions

Ways to ask the questions

Meaning: What does _____ mean?
(or)
What is the meaning of _____?

Spelling: How do you spell _____?
(or)
What is the spelling of _____?

Pronunciation: How do you pronounce _____?
(or)
What is the pronunciation of _____?

Translation: How do you say _____ in (language)?

Introductory Unit C: Basic Punctuation

Begin a sentence with a capital letter. End a sentence with a period.
Example: The capital of Sweden is Stockholm.

Begin a question with a capital letter. End a question with a question mark.
Example: Where do you live?

Use capital letters for names, cities, companies, countries, nationalities, languages, days, months, titles of books and movies, and the word *I*.

Examples: names: Daniel, Gabriel Bertot
cities: London, Tokyo
companies: National Trading Company
countries/nationalities: China, Brazil, Chinese, Brazilian
languages: English, French
days/months: Sunday, Wednesday, January, August
titles: the Quran, *Titanic*

Use a period after *Mr.* (a married man or a single man), *Mrs.* (a married woman), *Ms.* (a married woman or a single woman), and *Dr.*
Examples: Ms. Thompson, Mr. Chen, Dr. Harris

Use a comma between a date and a year. In the United States, the order of a date is month, date, and year.
Example: March 15, 1978

Another way to write the date is with numbers for month/date/year.
Example: March 15, 1978 = 3/15/78

Use a comma between a city and state or country.
Examples: Los Angeles, California
        Jakarta, Indonesia

Write the dollar sign ($) before the amount.
Put a period between dollars and cents.
Example: twenty-five dollars and fifty cents = $25.50

Use a colon to write the time.
Examples: 8:30, 1:20 a.m.

Introductory Unit D: Questions and Question Words

Three basic kinds of questions are *yes/no, or,* and *wh-* questions.

Yes/no questions
Examples: Are you a student? Yes, I am.
        Is Guatemala a very big country? No, it isn't.

Or questions
Examples: Are you from Latvia or Lithuania? I am from Latvia.
        Is Turkey in Europe or in Asia? It is in both.

Wh- questions
Examples: What is your name? My name is Youssef.
        When is your birthday? It is March 22.
        Why are you sad? I'm sad because my dog is sick.

Some basic question words
    who   what   when   why   which   how

Some examples of phrasal question words
    what time   what color   how far   how much   how many   how tall

**The first person singular subject pronoun is *I*. *I* comes before a verb.
In a question, *I* comes after the verb *be*.**

Examples: I am a student. Am I in the right place?

**The first person singular possessive adjective is *my*.
My comes before a noun.**

Example: My mother is a computer programmer.

**Me is an object pronoun. It comes after a verb (but not the verb *be*)
or a preposition.**

Examples: Please call me.
        Wait for me.

**The second person pronoun, singular and plural, subject and object,
is *you*. *You* comes before or after a verb and after a preposition.**

Examples: You are a good friend.
        I will call you.
        Is John with you?

**The second person possessive adjective is *your*. *Your* comes
before a noun.**

Examples: Where is your home?
        How is your class?

Unit 2: Subject Pronouns

Here are the subject pronouns.

I	we
you (singular)	you (plural)
he (masculine)	
she (feminine)	they
it (neuter)	

**Complete sentences in English have a subject. Nouns and pronouns
can be subjects.**

Examples: Pizza is a popular food.
        (*Pizza* is the subject.)

        It is delicious.
        (*It* is the subject.)

        Maria and Carmen are from Mexico.
        (*Maria and Carmen* is the subject.)

A complete sentence has to have a subject.
Incorrect: ~~Is hot~~ today.
Correct: It is hot today.
Exception: Imperatives have an implied subject *you.*
Examples: (You) Be careful!
            (You) Help me, please.

Do not use both a noun and its subject pronoun in a single sentence.
Incorrect: ~~Maria she~~ is from Mexico.
Correct: Maria is from Mexico. (or) She is from Mexico.

Unit 3: Singular and Plural Nouns

Add *-s* to most nouns to make a plural.
Examples: one book—two books
            a car—three cars

Some nouns have irregular plurals.
Examples: one child—four children
            a man—five men
            one woman—three women
            one person—two persons (or) two people
            one knife—many knives

0 (zero) books = no books

Adjectives do not take a plural ending.
Example: a big dog—two big dogs

Some nouns do not take a plural form. These nouns are called
noncount nouns **(see Unit 11).**
Examples: information, money, water

If a noun ends in *y* preceded by a consonant,
change the *y* to *i* and add *es* to make a plural.
Example: a country—a lot of countries

If a noun ends in *ch, s, sh,* or *x,* add *-es* to make a plural.
Examples: fox—foxes
            loss—losses
            dish—dishes
            watch—watches

Unit 4: Adjectives

Adjectives describe nouns. Adjectives usually come before nouns.
Examples: the big house, friendly people

Adjectives have no plural form.
Example: an expensive car—two expensive cars

Use an article only when there is a noun.
Incorrect: She is ~~a~~ rich.
　　　　 They are ~~the~~ small.
Correct: She is a rich woman.
　　　　 These are the small rooms.

Adjectives are not verbs. Every sentence must have a verb.
Incorrect: ~~My teachers nice.~~
　　　　　 ~~Russia big.~~
Correct: My teachers are nice.
　　　　 Russia is big.

Adjectives often follow the verb *be*.
Examples: Horses are fast.
　　　　 It is hot in the summer.

Some adjectives end in *-ed* and *-ing*, like *tired* and *interesting*.
Examples: The baby is tired.
　　　　 I am interested in art.
　　　　 That is an interesting book.

In a question, the word order is verb *be* + subject + adjective.
Examples: Is your apartment quiet?
　　　　 Are they cheap or expensive?

Unit 5: Demonstratives: *This, That, These, Those*

The four demonstratives are *this, that, these,* and *those*.
The demonstratives have different meanings.
　　　 this = singular—near speaker, here
　　　 that = singular—away from speaker, there
　　　 these = plural—near speaker, here
　　　 those = plural—away from speaker, there
　　　 Examples: This is an interesting book.
　　　　　　　 (The book is here, near the speaker)

　　　　　　　 Those police officers over there are friendly.
　　　　　　　 (The police officers are away from the speaker.)

Demonstratives can be used as pronouns or adjectives.
Pronouns: *this/that/these/those* + verb
Adjectives: *this/that/these/those* + noun
Examples: That is my car.
These are expensive.
This movie is great!
Those stories are funny.

A demonstrative pronoun is often used when introducing someone near the speaker.
Example: **Roberto:** This is my wife, Susanna.
Lee: Nice to meet you, Susanna.

Unit 6: The Verb *Be*

Every sentence has a verb. A common one is the verb *be*.
In the present tense, the verb *be* takes different forms.

I am	we are
you are (singular)	you are (plural)
he/she/it is	they are

Examples: I am a student.
You are very helpful.
My aunt is a good cook.
It is cold today.
We are all present today.
Roses are beautiful.

The verb *be* is often followed by an adjective, a noun, or a prepositional phrase.
Examples: Soda is sweet.
(verb *be* + adjective)

It's a game.
(verb *be* + noun)

The Eiffel Tower is in Paris.
(verb *be* + prepositional phrase)

A common mistake is to omit the verb *be*.
Incorrect: ~~My car red.~~
Correct: My car is red.

Contractions with _be_ are often used, especially in spoken English.

I am = I'm	we are = we're
you are = you're	you are = you're
he is = he's	
she is = she's	they are = they're
it is = it's	

Examples: I'm a student.

He's 20 years old.

It's cold today.

We're in class now.

You're all good teachers.

They're beautiful.

Unit 7: Negative of the Verb _Be_

To form the negative, put the word _not_ after the verb _be_.

Incorrect: ~~I not am tired.~~

Correct: I am not tired.

The negative of the verb _be_ is often followed by an adjective, a noun, or a prepositional phrase.

Examples: The moon is not hot. It is cold.
(negative of _be_ + adjective)

Damascus is not a new city.
(negative of _be_ + noun)

Mr. and Mrs. Evans are not from England.
(negative of _be_ + prepositional phrase)

Every sentence has a verb.

Incorrect: ~~He not at home.~~

Correct: He is not at home.

Do not confuse _no_ and _not_.

Incorrect: ~~They are no friendly.~~

Correct: They are not friendly.

Contractions of the negative of the verb *be* are often used.

I am not = I'm not

you are not = you're not	(or)	you aren't
he/she/it is not = he's not	(or)	he isn't
we are not = we're not	(or)	we aren't
they are not = they're not	(or)	they aren't

Examples: I'm not hungry.

She isn't here now.

She's not here now.

We aren't ready.

We're not ready.

They aren't new.

They're not new.

Unit 8: Prepositions of Time: *In, At, On*

Prepositions are followed by nouns.

Examples: in the morning, on Tuesday

The main prepositions of time are *in, at,* and *on.* Each preposition is used with different time expressions.

Examples: times: at 10:00 p.m., at 6:30, at midnight (12 o'clock at night)

days: on Monday, on Fridays, on the first day

dates: on June 5, on October 15, 1979

holidays: on Christmas, on Easter

seasons: in the winter, in the fall

months/years: in March, in July, in 2001, in 1996

periods of the day: in the morning, in the evening, at night

Plural time expressions

Example: I have karate class on Saturdays. (= every Saturday)

Combined time expressions

Examples: at 3:00 in the afternoon

on Saturday night

No prepositions are used with some expressions.

Examples: every day, every year

today, tomorrow

tonight, last night, tomorrow night

next week, last week

now

Prepositions of time can come at the beginning, middle, or end of a sentence.

Examples: In the winter, it is cold in Canada.

It is cold in the winter in Canada.

It is cold in Canada in the winter.

Another preposition of time: *during*

Example: during the week

Unit 9: *Yes/No* and *Or* Questions with the Verb *Be*

To form a sentence with the verb *be*, **use this word order: subject + verb.**

To form *yes/no* **and** *or* **questions with the verb** *be,* **use this word order: verb + subject.**

Examples: Are you a student? Yes, I am. I am a student.

Are Japanese cars big? No, they aren't. They are small.

Is Senegal in East Africa? No, it isn't. It is in West Africa.

Is Iran a Muslim or a Christian country? It is a Muslim country.

Short affirmative answers (Contractions are not used in short affirmative answers.)

Yes, I am.	Yes, we are.
Yes, you are. (singular)	Yes, you are. (plural)
Yes, he/she/it is.	Yes, they are.

Short negative answers and contractions

No, I am not.	(or)	No, I'm not.			
No, you are not.	(or)	No, you're not.	(or)	No, you aren't.
No, he is not.	(or)	No, she's not.	(or)	No, it isn't.
No, we are not.	(or)	No, we're not.	(or)	No, we aren't.
No, they are not.	(or)	No, they're not.	(or)	No, they aren't.

The answer to an *or* **question is not** *yes/no.*

Example: Is an elephant big or small?

Incorrect: ~~Yes, it is.~~

Correct: It is big.

Unit 10: *Wh-* Questions with the Verb *Be*

Some basic *wh-* **question words**

| who | what | where | when | why | which | how |

Some *wh-* **words are combined with other words to make questions:**

| what time | what color | how far | how long |
| how many | how much | how tall | |

To form *wh-* questions with the verb *be,* use this word order:
question word + verb *be* + subject.
Examples: Where are you from?
　　　　　When is the meeting?
　　　　　Who is your teacher?

In some cases, the question word or phrase is the subject
of the sentence.
Examples: Who is next to the door?
　　　　　What countries are near your country?
　　　　　How many students are in your class?

Unit 11: Count and Noncount Nouns: *A/An, Some, Any*

There are two kinds of nouns: count nouns and noncount nouns.

Count nouns have singular and plural forms.
Examples: car—cars
　　　　　pen—pens

Noncount nouns have only a singular form.

advice	crime	ice	love	milk	oil	time
air	food	information	mail	money	rice	traffic
coffee	furniture	jewelry	meat	music	smoke	water

**Use *a* or *an* with singular nouns. Do not use *a* or *an*
with plural nouns or noncount nouns.**
Correct: 　a book
　　　　　an umbrella
　　　　　information (noncount noun)
Incorrect: ~~a books~~
　　　　　~~an information~~

**Use *an* when the next word begins with *a, e, i, o,*
and *u* (when *u* has a vowel sound).**
Examples: an apple
　　　　　an open door
　　　　　a university (*U* sounds like the consonant *y.*)

Don't use *a/an* with proper nouns.
Incorrect: ~~Mr. Thomas is in a Paris.~~
Correct: 　Mr. Thomas is in Paris.

A and *an* are followed by a noun or an adjective + a noun.
Don't use *a/an* **with adjectives only.**
Correct: Alaska is a cold state.   (or)   Alaska is cold.
Incorrect: ~~Alaska is a cold.~~

Use *some* **with plural count nouns and singular noncount nouns.**
Examples: some students, some fruit

Any **is followed by plural count nouns and singular noncount nouns.**
Examples: any classes, not any women, any water

Use *any* **with negatives and questions.**
Examples: Are there any Americans in your class?
There are not any American students in our class.

Use *many* **with plural count nouns. Use** *much* **with noncount nouns.**
A lot of **is used with both count and noncount nouns.**
Correct: many boxes   (or)   a lot of boxes
          much gold   (or)   a lot of gold
Incorrect: ~~much boxes~~
          ~~many gold~~

Unit 12: *There Is* and *There Are*

Use T*here is/There are* **to express location, presence, or existence.**
Examples: There is a new computer lab at school.
There are a lot of excellent museums in New York.

There is **is followed by a singular subject.**
There are **is followed by a plural subject.**
Examples: There is an interesting program on TV tonight.
There are two kinds of elephants, African and Indian.

If there are two subjects, make the verb singular or plural
to match the first subject (the one closest to the verb).
Examples: There is a Mexican student and two Korean students in my class.
There are two Korean students and a Mexican student in my class.

Question form: *Is there . . . ?/Are there . . . ?*
Examples: Is there a museum in this town?
How many people are there in the class?

Negative forms: *There is not . . ./There are not . . .*
or *There is no . . ./There are no . . .*
Examples: There is no river in Rio de Janeiro.
There isn't a river in Rio de Janeiro.
There are no rivers in Rio de Janeiro.
There are not any rivers in Rio de Janeiro.

**There is and There are are usually followed by a noun,
not an adjective alone.**
Example: There is a supermarket behind the apartment.
Incorrect: ~~There is open.~~
Correct: It is open on Sundays.

**There is and It is are different. There is expresses existence or
location. The word *it* in It is usually refers to something that you
talked about already.**
Examples: There is a famous mountain in Japan called Mount Fuji.
It (= Mount Fuji) is very tall.

**There is and There are (meaning existence or location) are not usually
followed by *the*.**
Incorrect: ~~There is the refrigerator in my apartment.~~
(This sentence has a different meaning. It means that you are in the
apartment, pointing to the refrigerator.)
Correct: There is a refrigerator in my apartment.

Unit 13: Imperatives

**The imperative in English gives a command. It uses the simple form
of the verb.**
Examples: Come here!
Stand up!
Be quiet!

The implied subject of an imperative is *you*.
Example: Speak English! = You speak English.

**Please makes a sentence polite and can come at the beginning
(with no comma) or the end of a sentence (after a comma.)**
Examples: Please come here.
Stand up, please.
Be quiet, please.

The negative is formed with *do not (don't)* + verb.

Examples: Do not eat so fast.

Please don't tell anyone.

Don't be sad.

Use the verb *be* with an adjective.

Examples: Be careful!

Don't be late!

An exclamation point (!) with imperatives adds emphasis.

Examples: Listen to me! This is very important.

Don't do that! It's dangerous.

Unit 14: Present Tense of Verbs

Form of present tense verbs

I study	we go
you (one person) play	you (more than one person) play
he has	
she works	they read and study
it rains	

The present tense expresses something that happens habitually or is generally true. Time expressions that express regular action or habit are often used with the present tense.

Examples: I study every night.

You play soccer well.

He has black hair.

She works very hard.

It rains a lot in London.

We sometimes go bowling on the weekend.

Some people smoke when they drink coffee.

They never call us. They always send e-mail.

The third person singular form of the present tense ends in *s*.

Examples: he wants, she drives, it has

Do not use the verb *be* when expressing the simple present of other verbs. Never use the verb *be* together with the simple form of other verbs.

Incorrect: ~~I am speak English.~~

Correct: I speak English.

Unit 15: Present Tense: Third Person Singular -s

The third person singular present tense of verbs ends in s.
Examples: The teacher speaks English in class.
          She speaks English in class.

The third person singular present of the verb *have* is *has*.
Examples: My classmate has an English book.
          He has an English book.

If a verb ends in *e*, add -s to form the third person singular present tense.
Examples: take—takes
        write—writes

If a verb ends in *o, s, x, sh*, or *ch*, add -es.
Examples: watch—watches
        push—pushes
        go—goes
        mix—mixes
        pass—passes

If a verb ends in *y* preceded by a consonant, change *y* to *i*, and add -es.
Examples: study—studies
        carry—carries

If a verb ends in *y* preceded by a vowel, just add -s.
Examples: play—plays
        say—says

Unit 16: Present Tense: *Be* and Other Verbs

Every complete sentence in English has a verb, either the verb *be* or another verb.

Sentences with the verb *be*
Examples: A mouse is small.
        (*be* + adjective that refers to the subject)

        Titanic is a long movie.
        (*be* + noun that refers to the subject)

        The Rockies are in North America.
        (*be* + prepositional phrase about the subject)

Sentences with other verbs

Examples: Frank sings.
(subject + the verb *sings*)

Dogs eat meat.
(subject + the verb *eat* + object {noun})

Some people speak fast.
(subject + the verb *speak* + adverb)

It often rains in Vancouver.
(subject + adverb + the verb *rains* + prepositional phrase)

Remember: Don't use the verb *be* with the simple present form of another verb.

Incorrect: ~~I am have a car.~~
~~She is like movies.~~

Correct: I have a car.
She likes movies.

Unit 17: Prepositions of Place

Prepositions of place tell location. Here are some common prepositions of place.

in	from	over	next to
at	near	above	behind
on	between	under	far from
to	in front of	below	

Some prepositions have two or three words.
Examples: next to, in front of

Prepositions come before nouns, noun phrases, or pronouns.
Examples: in Russia, at the library, next to him
Switzerland is between Germany and Italy.

Use *in* with cities, states, regions, and countries.
Examples: in Tokyo, in California, in England

Use *in* to mean "inside."
Examples: The money is in my pocket.
The toy is in the box.

Use *in* with rooms.
Examples: in the classroom, in the kitchen

Use *on* to mean "on top of" or "on the surface of."
Examples: The flowers are on the table.
The book is on the desk.

Use *on* with sides.
Examples: on the left side, on the right

Use *on* with streets and electronic media (TV/radio/Internet).
Examples: She lives on First Street.
The new program is on TV.

Use *at* with addresses.
Example: She lives at 456 East First Street.

**Use *at* with words for places, like *store, school, work,* and *home,*
when the meaning is "general location."**
Examples: I buy soccer shoes at the sporting goods store.
David is not at home. He is at school.

Use *to* for movement, often with verbs like *come* and *go.*
Examples: I go to school on Mondays, Wednesdays, and Fridays.
Please come to my party tomorrow.
Exceptions: After school, I go home.
Many people go on vacation in the summer.

Unit 18: Adverbs of Frequency

Here are some common adverbs of frequency.
always   usually   often   sometimes   seldom   rarely   never

Adverbs of frequency express how often something happens.
always (100% of the time)
usually (about 85%)
often (about 70%)
sometimes (about 50%)
rarely/seldom (about 10%)
never (0%)
Examples: It is always cold in winter in Russia. (100% of the time)
I sometimes get up before 6:00 a.m. (about 50% of the time)
My teacher never wears shorts in class. (0% of the time)

Adverbs of frequency usually come after the verb *be*.
Examples: I am always hungry in the morning.
They are never on time for class.

In questions with the verb *be*, adverbs of frequency
come after the subject.
Example: Is he always late for class?

Adverbs of frequency come before other verbs.
Examples: You often drink too much soda.
My roommate usually watches TV in the evening.

The adverbs of frequency *often, usually,* and *sometimes*
can also come at the beginning of a sentence.
Examples: Sometimes my parents are angry with me.
Usually I walk my dog early in the morning.

Questions about frequency use the phrase *How often . . . ?*
Examples: How often do you eat out at restaurants? I eat out once a week.
How often are you late for class? I am usually on time for class.

Unit 19: Possessive Adjectives and Possessive Nouns

Possessive forms express ownership or relationship. There are
possessive adjectives and possessive forms of nouns.

Possessive adjectives are related to pronouns.
I—my
you—your
he—his
she—her
it—its
we—our
they—their

Possessive adjectives are followed by nouns, either singular or plural.
Examples: my country, my books
your teacher, your neighbors
his house, his eyes
her job, her parents
its size, its colors
our class, our friends
their car, their children
I have two brothers. Their names are Patrick and Dennis.
We study English. Our teacher is from Canada.
Mrs. Yamamoto lives in Tokyo, but her son lives in Osaka.

**Don't confuse the possessive adjective *its*
with the contraction *it's* (= *it is*).**
Don't confuse *their* with *there*.
Examples: China is an old country. Its history is very long.
   It's hot today.
   Mohammed and Fatima live in Chicago with their children.
   In Japan, there is a big holiday in August.

Possessive nouns are followed by other nouns, either singular or plural.
Examples: Josh owns a house. That is Josh's house.
   Sandy has twin boys. Sandy's babies are two months old.

Possessive nouns are used for both people and things.
Examples: my country's flag, today's newspaper

The possessive question word is *Whose*.
Example: Whose book is this? It is Roberto's book.

To make the possessive form of most nouns, add *'s* ("apostrophe *s*").
Examples: Jorge—Jorge's wife
   the teacher—the teacher's glasses
   the children—the children's teacher

If the singular form of the noun ends in *s*, add *'s* or just *'*.
Example: Thomas—Thomas's car (or) Thomas' car
   (Both forms are pronounced the same way.)

For plural nouns that end in *s*, just add *'*.
Examples: four students—four students' tests
   her parents—her parents' home
   (These forms are pronounced like the plural noun.)

**If two nouns possess one thing together, put the *'s*
only on the second noun.**
Example: Mr. Patel and Ms. Jameson run a grocery store.
   Mr. Patel and Ms. Jameson's store is big.

If two nouns possess two different things, put *'s* on both nouns.
Example: Alex's and Margo's computers are both in the classroom.

Unit 20: *Yes/No* and *Or* Questions with Present-Tense Verbs

Review of word order in *yes/no* and *or* questions with the verb *be*:
verb *be* + subject
Examples: Are you a student? Yes, I am.
             Is she here today? No, she isn't.
             Are they at the library now? Yes, they are.
             Am I on time, or am I late? You're on time.
             Is the meeting today or tomorrow? It's today.
             Are you hungry or not? I'm hungry.

***Do/Does* in questions with other verbs**

Do I . . . ?	Do we . . . ?
Do you . . . ?	Do you . . . ?
Does he/she/it . . . ?	Do they . . . ?

***Yes/no* and *or* questions with other verbs: *do/does* + subject + verb**
Examples: Do you have a car? Yes, I do.
             Does he speak English? No, he doesn't.
             Do they usually eat at the cafeteria? Yes, they do.
             Do you walk to school or take the bus? I take the bus.
             Does she like classical music or rock? She likes rock.
             Do we have class at 8:00 or at 9:00? At 9:00.

Short answers to *yes/no* questions
Yes, I/you/we/they do.   No, I/you/we/they don't.
Yes, he/she/it does.   No, he/she/it doesn't.

Do not use *do/does* with the verb *be*.
Incorrect: ~~Do you are tired?~~
Correct: Are you tired?

Do not use the verb *be* with the simple form of other verbs.
Incorrect: ~~Are you speak English?~~
Correct: Do you speak English?

Unit 21: *Wh-* Questions with Present-Tense Verbs

Some basic *wh-* question words

who	whom	what	where	what color	what kind	how many
when	why	which	how	what time	how much	

Word order in present-tense questions with verbs other than *be*:
wh- question word + *do/does* + subject + simple form of the verb
Examples: Where do you live?

          What time does the train arrive?

In questions, the subject never immediately follows the *wh*- word.
Incorrect: ~~Why you like this movie?~~

          ~~Where he works?~~

Correct: Why do you like this movie?

          Where does he work?

Use *do* with *I, you, we,* and *they*. Use *does* with *he, she,* and *it*.
Examples: What do I . . . ?

          Why does he . . . ?
          How do you . . . ?
          Whom does she . . . ?
          Where do we . . . ?
          What time does it . . . ?
          When do they . . . ?

**If the question word is the subject or part of the subject,
do not use *do/does*. Use question word + verb.**
Examples: Who knows the answer?

          How many students come every day?

Do not use *do/does* together with the verb *be*.
Examples: When is the class?

          (verb *be* with a noun)

          When are you usually hungry?
          (verb *be* with an adjective)

Use *do/does* with other verbs.
Examples: When does the class begin?

          (verb *begin*)

          When do you usually get hungry?
          (verb *get*)

Who is used as the subject of a question. *Whom* is used as an object of a verb or a preposition. *Whom* is more formal. In casual speech, *who* is often used as an object.

Examples: Who has your book?
(*Who* is the subject.)

Whom do you wish to see?
(*You* is the subject. *Whom* is the object.)

Unit 22: Present-Tense Negative Verbs

Negative present tense of the verb *be*

I am not	we are not
you are not	you are not
he/she/it is not	they are not

Examples of negative present tense of other verbs

I do not run	we do not want
you do not like	you do not go
he/she/it does not have	they do not need

Always use the simple form of the verb after *do/does not.*
Incorrect: She does not ~~smokes~~.
Correct: She does not smoke.

Negative sentences with the verb *be*
Examples: We are not ready for the test.
(negative of the verb *be* with an adjective)

That room is not the kitchen.
(negative of the verb *be* with a noun)

Tokyo is not in China.
(negative of the verb *be* with a prepositional phrase)

Negative sentences with other verbs
Examples: We do not understand the grammar.
(negative of the verb *understand* with the subject *we*)

A new baby does not have any teeth.
(negative of the verb *have* with the subject *baby*)

Unit 23: Present Progressive Tense

Review: The simple present expresses a habitual action, something that is generally true.

Examples: My parents get home from work every day at about 6:30 p.m.

It snows a lot in Finland in December.

I don't cook very much.

The present progressive expresses something that is (or is not) happening right now.

Examples: It isn't snowing right now.

My daughter is cooking now.

My parents are working today.

Some verbs do not usually use the present progressive. They use the simple present to refer to something that is happening right now.

| believe | have | know | need | see | remember | look (appearance) |
| forget | hear | like | love | want | understand | |

Examples: I hear a train. (right now)

He looks tired. (right now)

Do you understand this? (right now)

She doesn't have her book. (right now)

Exceptions: What are you looking at?

I'm having some difficulty.

To form the present progressive, use the appropriate form of the verb *be* + verb + *-ing*. Contractions are often used in speaking.

Examples: I am studying now.   (or)   I'm studying now.

You are making a mistake.   (or)   You're making a mistake.

She is not coming today.   (or)   She isn't coming today.

It is getting dark.   (or)   It's getting dark.

We are not worrying about it. (or)   We aren't worrying about it.

They are waiting for the bus. (or)   They're waiting for the bus.

Remember: Do not use the simple form of the verb after the verb *be*.

Incorrect: ~~They are practice right now.~~

Correct: They are practicing right now.

Question formation: Use the verb *be* + subject + verb + *-ing*.

Examples: Are you listening to me? Yes, I am.

What is he doing? He's doing his homework.

When adding *-ing* to one-syllable verbs ending with a single vowel and a single consonant, double the final consonant.

Examples: stop—stopping

win—winning

For one-syllable verbs ending in two vowels and a consonant, just add *-ing.*

Examples: clean—cleaning

rain—raining

For verbs ending with a consonant and a single *e,* drop the *e* and add *-ing.*

Examples: lose—losing

change—changing

For verbs ending in the letter *y,* just add *-ing.*

Examples: say—saying

carry—carrying

For verbs ending in *ie,* drop the *ie* and add *-ying.*

Examples: die—dying

lie—lying

For two-syllable verbs with the stress on the first syllable and ending in a single vowel and a single consonant, add *-ing.*

Examples: happen—happening

listen—listening

For two-syllable verbs with the stress on the second syllable and ending in a single vowel and a single consonant, double the final consonant and add *-ing.*

Examples: occur—occurring

refer—referring

Unit 24: Connectors: *And, But, Or, So*

The connectors *and, but, or,* and *so* have different meanings.

And expresses addition or combination. It means "also."

But expresses contrast or difference.

Or indicates choice or different possibilities.

So introduces a result.

And, but, and *or* connect adjectives, nouns, and verbs.

Examples: The streets are crowded and noisy.
(adjective *and* adjective)

He comes to school with his father or mother.
(noun *or* noun)

She loves coffee but hates soda.
(verb *but* verb)

The boys like soccer but do not like baseball.
(verb *but* negative verb)

And and *or* can connect more than two words. Put a comma
after each word except the last one.

Examples: George works with Tomas, Ernesto, and Susan.
They are serving coffee, tea, soda, or water with the meal.

And, but, or, and *so* connect sentences, or clauses (subject + verb).
Usually, there is a comma before the connector:
subject + verb, *and/but/or/so* subject + verb

Examples: Russia is a big country, and it has a lot of resources.
I usually read in the evening, but tonight I'm watching a movie.
At night, we eat at home, or we go to a restaurant.
My friend has a lot of children, so she lives in a big house.

Unit 25: Past Tense

To make the past tense of regular verbs, add *-ed.*
Examples: walk—walked
answer—answered

With verbs ending in a consonant and the letter *e,* add *-d.*
Examples: change—changed
smile—smiled

With verbs ending in *ie,* add *-d.*
Examples: die—died
lie—lied

With one-syllable verbs ending in a single vowel and single consonant, double the final consonant (except *w*, *x*, or *y*) and add *-ed*.

Examples: fan—fanned
stop—stopped

Exceptions: box—boxed
show—showed
stay—stayed

With verbs ending in a consonant + *y*, change the *y* to *i* and add *-ed*.

Examples: carry—carried
try—tried

With two-syllable verbs with the stress on the first syllable and ending in a single vowel and single consonant, add *-ed*.

Examples: happen—happened
listen—listened

With two-syllable verbs with the stress on the second syllable and ending in a single vowel and single consonant, double the final consonant and add *-ed*.

Examples: occur—occurred
prefer—preferred

Some regular verbs

answered	closed	jumped	needed	stayed	washed
asked	cooked	killed	opened	turned	watched
believed	danced	liked	played	visited	worked
called	entered	listened	rained	waited	
changed	finished	looked	showed	walked	
cleaned	helped	moved	started	wanted	

Present- and past-tense forms of some common irregular verbs

begin—began	forget—forgot	put—put	speak—spoke
break—broke	get—got	read—read	steal—stole
bring—brought	give—gave	run—ran	swim—swam
build—built	go—went	say—said	take—took
buy—bought	have—had	see—saw	teach—taught
come—came	hear—heard	sell—sold	tell—told
do—did	know—knew	send—sent	understand—understood
eat—ate	make—made	sing—sang	write—wrote
find—found	pay—paid	sit—sat	

To make the negative in the past tense, use *did not* + the simple form of the verb.

Incorrect: ~~Last night, we did not went to the party.~~
~~Yesterday, we did not studied at the library.~~

Correct: Last night, we did not go to the party.
Yesterday, we did not study at the library.

The contraction of *did not* is *didn't*.
Examples: I didn't do it.
They didn't need my help.

The past tense of the verb *be* is *was/were*.
Use *was* with *I* and with *he/she/it*.
Use *were* with *you, we*, and *they*.
Examples: I was in the house all night.
We were late.
You were right.
You were in the lab yesterday.
He was my teacher last year.
They were in class all day.

In the past tense, as in the present tense, the verb *be* can be followed by various structures.
Examples: I was tired yesterday.
(verb *be* + adjective)

Last night, we were at the movies.
(verb *be* + prepositional phrase)

My grandmother was a chemist.
(verb *be* + noun)

Negative forms and questions with the verb *be*

Negative	Question
I was not	Was I . . . ?
You were not	Were you . . . ?
He/She/It was not	Was he . . . ?
We were not	Were we . . . ?
You were not	Were you . . . ?
They were not	Were they . . . ?

Remember: Do not use the verb *be* with the simple form of verbs.
Incorrect: ~~Yesterday, I was have a test.~~
Correct: Yesterday, I had a test.

**The word *can* with a verb means ability, permission, or willingness.
The word *will* with a verb indicates future time.**

Use the simple form of the verb with *can* and *will*. Don't use *to*.

Incorrect: ~~I can to go with you.~~
~~We will to move next month.~~

Correct: I can go with you.
We will move next month.

In the negative, the word *not* comes after *can* or *will*. Use *not*. Do not use *no* in the negative.

Incorrect: ~~I no can do that.~~
~~It no will rain tomorrow.~~

Correct: I cannot do that.
It will not rain tomorrow.

**The contraction of *will* is *'ll*. The contraction of *cannot* is *can't*.
The contraction of *will not* is *won't*.**

Examples: I'll be there at 10:00.
We'll come tomorrow.
You can't do that.
You won't like this program.
He'll get a job next year.
They can't finish the homework.

Make questions by putting *can* or *will* in front of the subject.

Examples: Can you come to the party?
Will you buy a new computer?
When can I visit you?
Why will you be late?

Do not use *am/is/are* or *do/does* with *can* or *will*.

Incorrect: ~~They don't can speak German.~~
~~He doesn't will tell me.~~
~~Are you can play the piano?~~

Correct: They can't speak German.
He won't tell me.
Can you play the piano?

You must use a verb with *can* and *will*, not just an adjective or a noun.

Incorrect: ~~I will absent tomorrow.~~
~~He can't Spanish very well.~~

Correct: I will be absent tomorrow.
He can't speak Spanish very well.